SUPERFOOD JUICING

SUPERFOOD JUICING

Nutritious and Vitamin-Rich Recipes to Supercharge Your Health

NORA DAY

ROCKRIDGE
PRESS

For general information on our other products and services, please contact our Customer Care Department within the United States at (866) 744-2665, or outside the United States at (510) 253-0500.

Some of the recipes originally appeared, in different form, in *Green Juicing Diet, Juicing, Juicing for Beginners, The Complete Juicing Recipe Book, The Juicing Recipes Book, The 5-Day Juicing Diet, Juicing for Health, The Green Juicing Recipe Book, The Juicing Diet*, and *Juice Cleanse Recipes*.

Paperback ISBN: 978-1-63807-791-6
eBook ISBN: 978-1-68539-153-9

Manufactured in the United States of America

Interior and Cover Designer: Amanda Kirk
Art Producer: Sara Feinstein
Editor: Leah Zarra
Production Editor: Emily Sheehan
Production Manager: David Zapanta

Photography © Shutterstock.com, cover, back cover and p. V; © Marc Tran/Stocksy, pp. II, 22, 88; © Hélène Dujardin, p. VIII © Evi Abeler, p. 16 (all except upper right); © Ray Kachatorian, p. 16 (upper right); © Pixel Stories/Stocksy, pp. 44, 66; © Juan Moyano/Stocksy, p. 110

10 9 8 7 6 5 4 3 2 1 0

Contents

Introduction

Welcome to the vibrant, healthy lifestyle of juicing with superfoods. I'm Nora Day, and I have been juicing every single day for more than thirty years—I guess you could say juicing is my passion! Juicing changed my life by adding more confidence, ease, patience, productivity, and clarity and an overall consistent wellness routine to my mind and body. Getting into the habit of juicing with superfoods is an easy, positive way to feed your body, mind, and soul with overwhelming goodness. I look forward to my daily juice because I know I am taking care of myself exponentially by consuming the active properties of superfoods. I wrote *Superfood Juicing* so you can benefit from and enjoy the healthy improvements a juicing lifestyle has to offer. From a high nutrition value to heightened awareness and energy to glowing skin, juicing superfoods is a well-balanced approach to greater health, longevity, and well-being.

Why are superfoods so amazing to add to your juices? The vitamins, minerals, and antioxidants that are packed into superfoods deliver maximum nutritional benefits for minimal calories. Instead of feeling bloated, lethargic, or as if you're in a food coma from overeating, you will love the satisfied feeling of your mind and body working in harmony to receive such a healthy, positive liquid infusion in just one superfood juice serving. Juicing with superfoods can be convenient, easy, and (above all) delicious. Think of the recipes in this book as a primary step to your daily intake of superfoods.

Superfood juicing can be an "every day" wellness ritual in your life, which you can accomplish by simply following the recipes in this book. You will notice a higher level of energy, more glow and brightness to your skin, fewer aches and pains, and a balanced, peaceful mind-body connection. Superfood juices help you maintain a focused energy throughout a workout, busy day, or business meeting and will give you a happily nourished body with fewer calories than most meals. As your body and mind continually receive refreshing superfood juices, you are able to concentrate and center your attention without distraction, feel less stress, and become more aware and attentive to what's truly important to you. Think of superfood juicing as unclogging and polishing your senses for more clarity. Natural beauty is magnified and brought into focus through the infusion of superfoods so you can fully appreciate the colors of the sky, the sounds of the birds, and the smells of the sea or clean mountain air. I firmly believe juicing with superfoods can change your life for the better when you follow the recipes in *Superfood Juicing*.

But keep in mind that you should not consume only juices, no matter how good they are for you. There is so much other delicious, healthy food to add into your balanced and healthy lifestyle—juices are just your starting point. I encourage you to speak with your doctor if a plant-based juicing routine is a drastic change in your diet.

—

CHAPTER 1

GET *SUPER* INTO JUICE

I PUT THIS CHAPTER TOGETHER TO MAKE IT SIMPLE, informative, and easy to jump into a juicing routine and also to answer some of your questions and concerns. By simplifying all aspects of superfood juicing, you will have a broader understanding of the enormous benefits of daily juicing. Identifying which machine is best for your lifestyle, with pros and cons, and providing lists of superfood vegetables, leafy greens, and fruits are some of the many highlights of this chapter. The first topic we address is why you should juice. Read on to find out why!

WHY JUICE?

Juicing machines extract only the juice from fruits and vegetables, and that juice is full of potent vitamins, minerals, and antioxidants—without the fiber. When you consume these fresh juices, the nutrients are absorbed into your body quickly, and your digestive system gets a rest from digesting fiber. Daily juicing helps remove toxins from your body, boosts your immune system, and can also help you lose weight. The low-calorie intake of a single serving of juice and the appetite satisfaction your tummy and brain feel add up to a healthy, light, nutritious juice, replacement meal, or snack.

People turn to juicing for a variety of health and convenience reasons. Juicing is a wonderful addition to your already healthy diet or a positive option if you would like to become healthier by consuming more fruits and vegetables. Here are the five most common reasons I have seen people turn to juicing—with great results!

On-the-go, time-saving meals. Juicing is the at-home, at-work, on-the-go, healthy take-out alternative. A flavorful juice is a great way to start your busy morning.

Lighter body and mind. Losing a few pounds and feeling lighter in the body is a positive side effect from juicing, which can offer more self-confidence, self-love, and self-appreciation to your mind.

The great reset. Juicing is an easy, effective way to reset, recharge, and receive a fresh start to a healthy lifestyle. The high amounts of vitamins, minerals, and antioxidants from juicing uplift and energize from the inside out.

Glowing skin. The largest organ you have is your skin. The living, raw, organic fruits and vegetables used for juicing encourage glowing skin through the cleansing effect of drinking superfood juices.

More plants. Increasingly, people are looking to add more fruits and vegetables to their diet for health reasons. Juices are packed with fruits and vegetables for an easy transition to a more plant-based diet.

SUPERFOODS DEFINED

There is sometimes confusion and controversy around the term "superfood." Superfoods are super-charged, healthy foods for your body and mind. When you receive maximal nutritional benefits through foods with high vitamin, mineral, and antioxidant levels, you are having a superfood! These foods are mostly plant-based, natural, nutritionally dense foods like avocado, beets, berries, dark leafy greens, ginger, nuts, and seeds. The nutrient-dense quality of the ingredients in this book makes you feel full, quenched, and satisfied with smaller portions, which can encourage weight loss even as you receive profound amounts of vitamins and minerals.

Superfood Juicing is a perfect source of amazing superfood juice recipes you can incorporate into your diet and use to create a foundation of superfood knowledge. The recipes I have chosen for this book not only taste delicious but also are packed with superfood ingredients. Depending on the unique ingredient lists, you can benefit from feelings of mental clarity, experience more energy, or improve digestive health as you consistently boost your immune system. All recipes are intended to support and encourage a healthy lifestyle of superfood juicing.

Most of the fruits, nuts, seeds, and vegetables in this book are classified as superfoods because they are high in vitamins, minerals, and antioxidants and are in their raw, unprocessed state. All of nature's vitamins and minerals are intact because the ingredients aren't baked, steamed, or fried. This is why the superfoods in this book are so simple, approachable, and accessible. Superfoods are simply foods that are especially rich in nutrients and vitamins with the capacity to address a health need, encourage a healthier lifestyle, and keep your mind and body in tip-top condition. Many are foods you already know and see at your local market. Superfood juicing allows a healthy approach to a mind-body wellness journey.

SUPERFOOD JUICING BENEFITS

Juicing is a lifestyle. Most people don't consume enough fruits and vegetables in their day-to-day diets, which is why superfood juicing is such an important part of a vibrant, healthy, well-balanced diet. Juicing links more of those valuable superfood nutrients and vitamins immediately into your cells and can also satisfy your taste buds and your tummy enough that you might not want to reach for the prepackaged, processed snack. Weight loss is a possible positive upside to juicing regularly due to the lower calorie count in most juices compared with an alternative meal as well as the conscious awareness of healthy food choices.

Juicing superfoods exclusively isn't always an option, depending on what produce is in season and the availability of certain superfoods in your area. This is no excuse not to juice quality organic fruits and vegetables you do have, though! Stay on track with your juicing routine by making the recipes you can with the produce available. The benefit of nutrient-dense superfood ingredients such as bananas, blueberries, broccoli, and kale is that they are produce powerhouses. When you have the option to add superfoods, your juices are more nutrient-rich. That said, all fruits and vegetables, in their raw, living food state, are packed with beneficial vitamins, minerals, and enzymes that provide substantial health benefits.

The recipe chapters in this book are organized to help you find juices for the health benefits you're looking for.

Magic Morning

Chapter 2 is full of refreshing, eye-opening ingredients like cucumber, green tea, lemon, mint, and spinach. Drinking the superfood juices in this chapter, first thing in the morning on an empty stomach, offers high rewards. Your mind and body benefit by absorbing nutrients immediately as the fiber is extracted from the juice. If you have a sluggish digestive system, I recommend having a juice from this chapter two or three mornings every week. As your system quickly digests and assimilates your superfood juice, you gain more morning brainpower, more energy, and a fresh lightness to start your day.

Energy Surge

Whether you need extra midday energy or just want to enliven and bring more energy to your day, chapter 3 is for you. Ingredients like blueberries, broccoli, coconut water, and maca powder supply your cells, body, and mind with healthy, invigorating, energizing juices. From the hydrating, high-electrolyte properties in coconut water to the energy-boosting properties in maca powder, you will feel nourished and alert. Staying fully hydrated helps keep your mind and body fully energized. The superfood juices in this chapter are packed with high-energy, substantially hydrating ingredients to ensure that you function at your highest potential.

Green Juice

The green juices in chapter 4 are unique, delicious, and, yes, super green! Ingredients such as avocado, fennel bulb, kale, pistachios, and Swiss chard create powerful green beverages. According to the Harvard School of Public Health's *The Nutrition Source*, kale, often known as the king of greens, is rich in vitamins A, C, and K; calcium; potassium; and antioxidants. Dark leafy greens are nutrient-dense superfoods that give you vitamins, protein, and minerals and are low in calories. I recommend drinking a green juice three times a week to fast-track your healthy lifestyle. The infusion of valuable nutrients in these juices can bring more focus, consistency, and endurance to your workouts, meditations, and workdays.

Immune Booster

To fight off viral infections and stay healthy all year long, chapter 5 and its immune booster juices are here to save the day. Beet greens, beets, citrus, and ginger root are some of the powerful ingredients in this chapter. Antioxidants such as vitamin C help build your immune system so viral colds stay away, and this chapter is abundant in a variety of vitamin C sources. The mighty recipes in this chapter are healing, tasty juice tonics loaded with vitamins to build and sustain your immune system. Whether you are rebuilding your immune system from chronic ailments or supporting your general health, this chapter has a wonderful selection of recipes to reinforce your healthy lifestyle.

Cleanse and Detox

It's important to give yourself regular cleansing and detoxing love—from your digestive system to your skin. However, chapter 6 does not promote a juice cleanse but rather assists with a consistent, overall wellness routine. Ingredients such as apple, artichoke, celery, and turmeric will encourage cleansing that promotes regular elimination, clear thoughts, and healthy, glowing skin. The recipes in this chapter will keep you hydrated as you detox through their high water content and nutritional ingredient combinations. Specific ingredients, like artichoke and turmeric, were selected for healthy collagen development, which can give the gift of younger-looking skin.

Juicing with Care

Juicing is a fantastic option for busy, health-conscious people who want to ensure that they get sufficient daily intake of fruits and vegetables. It is also a great option for people who want to incorporate more fruits and vegetables into their diet and for people completely new to juicing who want to improve their overall health. In reviewing twenty-two studies, the National Institutes of Health found not only that drinking juice made from fresh fruits and vegetables improved folate and antioxidant levels, including beta-carotene and vitamins C and E, but also that this liquid form of produce may reduce homocysteine levels and markers of oxidative stress—all linked to improved heart health.

Though these results are certainly promising, more studies are needed to better understand the magnificent health effects of fruit and vegetable juicing. Juicing is not a proven cure-all or magic pill. Eating a well-balanced diet along with your juicing routine is recommended—the healthy juices in this book are just an added bonus to your healthy lifestyle journey. Please consult with a doctor before making any drastic changes to your diet.

TYPES OF JUICERS

Investing in a juicer is investing in your healthy lifestyle. Every juicer has its merits, and you should choose one that's most beneficial to your needs and budget. Some things you should consider before buying a juicer are the price, size, and noise level and whether you are a casual, passionate, or hardcore juicer.

Centrifugal Force Juicer

This is one of the most popular machines on the market, known for its quick and easy juicing capabilities. A sharp, fast-moving blade chops fruits and vegetables, and a mesh filter separates the pulp from the liquid. This model isn't as proficient as others at juicing leafy greens, but it is a powerful, solid machine. A lot of the nutrients from your produce end up in the high pulp content, and the heat from the fast-moving motor produces high oxidation levels, which means juices may not keep as long in the refrigerator. Casual or first-time juicers and busy people who want to juice but don't have a lot of time will benefit from this juicer.

PROS

- Affordable options
- Easy to use
- Less time chopping produce, as large pieces fit through the feeder
- Most fruits and vegetables juice easily
- Produces juice fast as you can quickly and continuously add produce

CONS

- High oxidation levels
- Juice less nutritionally valuable than with other models because of the heat used
- Juice has more foam and separates quickly
- Larger machines that take up more counter space and are harder to store
- Louder than other cold press models
- Produces a large amount of pulp and less juice than cold press models

Masticating Juicer (Slow Juicer)

The most attractive feature of this style of juicer is the higher nutrient level and amount of juice produced versus other models. Rather than a blade, slow juicers have an auger that slowly crushes and chews fruits and vegetables. The low-speed motor creates lower oxidation levels, so you can keep extra portions longer, and the slow juicer can handle a wider variety of fruits, vegetables, frozen produce, and nuts. The juice stays fresher longer in the refrigerator, is more potent, and yields a higher quantity and quality of juice with less pulp. If you are passionate about juicing and are currently juicing at home or plan to juice up to three or four times a week, the masticating juicer model is a good investment.

PROS

- Higher juice yield means extra portions for the next day
- Juice has less foam and is slow to separate
- Juice has more nutritional value because of the extraction process
- Produces a superior-tasting juice
- Quieter than other models
- Low oxidation levels
- Majority of produce is turned into juice; minimal produce waste means more value for your money

CONS

- Chopping and prep take longer because of the smaller juice feeder
- Cleaning the appliance is more time-consuming than other models
- Juicing process takes longer
- More expensive than other juicers

Triturating (Twin Gear Juicer)

The triturating juicer is also part of the masticating, slow-juicer family, but two stainless-steel augers set this juicer apart. Because of the twin gear feature, this juicer can also make soups and noodles, grind nuts and seeds, and chop vegetables. This industrial juicer is exceptional at separating the liquid from the hard fiber to make very high-yield, high-quality juices with a low oxidation level. It processes common fruit, leafy greens, root vegetables, nuts, and seeds with ease. The nutrient-dense juice produced stays fresher longer in the refrigerator without losing its potency. I recommend this juicer for dedicated, hardcore juicers who juice four or five days a week or more and prioritize a healthy lifestyle.

PROS

- Can process hard to soft produce, nuts, and seeds easily
- Five-year-plus warranty
- Has food processing functions
- Juice has less foam and is slow to separate
- Low oxidation levels
- Quieter than other models
- Users rate it best quality, best yield, and with least amount of pulp (waste)

CONS

- Heavy, bulky machine; not easy to move or store
- High price
- Takes longer to clean

Juice Press

This machine is unique in that it is the only juicer that contains a press, to warrant the name "cold press" juice. This two-stage juicer grinds the produce into pulp, and then the juice is extracted slowly by pressing the pulp under thousands of pounds of pressure. Because of this process, the juice press, hands down, extracts the most nutrients possible from fruits and vegetables. The purest juice, with almost zero waste (pulp), comes from a juice press machine. The juice press can also make dairy-free milks, like almond, hemp, macadamia, and oat. For hardcore juicers who want to experience the highest form of juicing, the juice press machine will satisfy your expectations.

PROS

- Achieves the highest yield, from leafy greens to root vegetables, and extracts the most nutrients possible

- Can also make nut and seed milks and nut oils

- Juice has little to no foam

- Longest shelf life—juices can be refrigerated for 3 to 5 days with little or no separation or breakdown of nutrient content

- Low oxidation levels

CONS

- Most expensive juicer

- Heavy, bulky machine; not easy to move, store, or clean

- Requires the use of reusable or limited-use press bags to hold the pulp

SUPERFOOD JUICE RATIOS

Superfoods are nutrient-rich, nutrient-dense, powerful additions to your juices, but you don't necessarily need to use a lot of a superfood to see benefits. Our bodies can only absorb and use a certain amount of each vitamin and nutrient. I have found when I load too many superfood ingredients into one juice, it ruins the flavor, and it is too harsh on my digestive system. On the next page are some helpful guidelines to create the best juices possible.

Storage

Self-appreciation, gratitude, and effort go into making juices, so they deserve to be stored properly. Storing leftover portions in an airtight glass container works best. Glass never exudes any residue odor, making it a top choice for storing your energy-filled juices. In these recipes, I give general storage recommendations for each juice—some keep longer than others because of the ingredients used and oxidation levels. The oxidation is the heat released by your juicer, which can degrade the nutrients in your juice. Slow juicers, like the masticating, cold press, and triturating juicers, produce low oxidation because their motors operate at a lower speed. Centrifugal juicers operate at a much higher speed and their juices tend to spoil more quickly.

Remember, you are preparing unpasteurized, living enzymes in a glass. Whenever possible, drink freshly made juices immediately after making them to enjoy their highest nutritional value. Having said that, it is still vastly superior to make your own juice and drink the extra portion the following day than to purchase store-bought juice, which has been on the shelf for at least 24 hours and, in some cases, up to 5 days.

SUPERFOOD	MINIMUM AMOUNT	MAXIMUM AMOUNT
VEGETABLES		
Arugula	¼ cup; 6 grams	1 cup; 24 grams
Avocado	½ medium avocado, ¼ cup diced; 37.5 grams	1 medium avocado, 1 cup diced; 150 grams
Beets	½ cup diced; 40 grams	2 cups diced; 160 grams
Bell pepper	¼ bell pepper, ¼ cup diced; 35.5 grams	1 bell pepper, 1 cup cubed; 142 grams
Bok choy	½ cup shredded; 35 grams	1 cup shredded; 70 grams
Broccoli	½ cup; 40.5 grams	2 cups; 162 grams
Butternut squash	½ cup diced; 102.5 grams	2 cups cubed; 410 grams
Cabbage	¼ cup shredded; 22.25 grams	1 cup shredded; 89 grams
Cauliflower	½ cup; 64 grams	2 cups; 256 grams
Chard	¼ cup shredded; 43.75 grams	1 cup shredded; 175 grams
Collard greens	¼ cup shredded; 47.5 grams	1 cup shredded; 190 grams
Kale	3 leaves; 15 grams	5 leaves; 25 grams
Parsnips	¼ cup cubed; 33.25 grams	1 cup cubed; 133 grams
Romaine lettuce	½ cup shredded; 37.5 grams	4 cups shredded; 300 grams
Spinach	½ cup; 15 grams	4 cups; 120 grams
FRUITS		
Acai	½ cup; 100 grams	1 cup; 200 grams
Apples	½ medium apple, ½ cup chopped; 60 grams	2 medium apples, 2 cups chopped; 240 grams
Bananas	1 medium; 118 grams	2 medium; 236 grams
Blueberries	½ cup; 75 grams	2 cups; 300 grams
Cherries	½ cup; 69 grams	2 cups; 276 grams
Cranberries	½ cup; 55 grams	2 cups; 220 grams
Grapes	½ cup; 75.5 grams	2 cups; 302 grams
Oranges	½ medium orange; 70 grams	3 medium oranges; 420 grams

SUPERFOOD	MINIMUM AMOUNT	MAXIMUM AMOUNT
Pineapple	½ cup cubed; 100 grams	2 cups cubed; 400 grams
Pomegranate	¼ cup; 35 grams	1 cup; 140 grams
Raspberries	½ cup; 61.5 grams	2 cups; 246 grams
Tomatoes	1 small tomato; 100 grams	4 small tomatoes; 400 grams
SPICES		
Cacao powder	1 teaspoon; 2.08 grams	4 teaspoons; 8.32 grams
Cinnamon, ground	½ teaspoon; 1.38 grams	2 teaspoons; 5.52 grams
Ginger, fresh	½-inch piece	2-inch piece
Ginger, ground	1 teaspoon; 2.81 grams	1 tablespoon; 8.43 grams
Maca powder	½ teaspoon; 2.49 grams	1 tablespoon; 14.94 grams
Spirulina powder	½ teaspoon; 1.5 grams	2 teaspoons; 6 grams
Turmeric root, fresh	½-inch piece	2-inch piece
Turmeric, ground	1 teaspoon; 3.18 grams	1 tablespoon; 9.54 grams
NUTS, SEEDS, AND GRAINS		
Almond butter	1 tablespoon; 15 grams	¼ cup; 60 grams
Almonds	¼ cup; 35.5 grams	½ cup; 71 grams
Chia seeds	1 teaspoon; 3.36 grams	4 teaspoons; 13.44 grams
Coconut water	½ cup; 120 grams	2 cups; 480 grams
Flaxseed	1 teaspoon; 3.11 grams	4 teaspoons; 12.44 grams
Oats	¼ cup; 24.75	1 cup; 99 grams
Pecan butter	1 tablespoon; 16 grams	¼ cup; 64 grams
Pecans	¼ cup; 28.25 grams	½ cup; 56.5 grams
Pistachio butter	1 tablespoon; 14 grams	¼ cup; 56 grams
Pistachios	¼ cup; 31 grams	½ cup; 62 grams
Pumpkin seed butter	1 tablespoon; 14 grams	¼ cup; 56 grams
Pumpkin seeds	¼ cup; 16 grams	½ cup; 32 grams

BUILDING BLOCKS OF A SUPERFOOD JUICE STASH

You will want to keep a basic stash of superfoods in your refrigerator (fresh produce), in your pantry (spices), and in airtight glass containers (nuts and seeds). There's nothing worse than wanting to make a superfood juice only to find you're missing an ingredient! There are specific fruits, leafy greens, nuts, vegetables, seeds, spices, and mix-ins that are go-to building blocks to stock your superfood kitchen. Fruits can help sweeten an intense green juice, whereas vegetables can aid a detox juice. Nuts and seeds provide extra protein, and spices can add medicinal qualities.

Superfood Fruits

Fruits add hydration and are energizing, refreshing ingredients when added to superfood juices. The antioxidant, vitamin, and mineral content found in these fruits lends to their superfood qualities, whereas the sweetness balances tart, earthy, spicy flavors. The color of juice does affect perceptions of taste. The bright colors of superfood fruits, like acai, blueberries, cranberries, and oranges, bring an uplifting, happy feeling that motivates good energy from digestion to an outer glow. Here are some of my favorite superfood fruits used in this book:

Acai	Blueberries	Pineapple
Apples	Cherries	Pomegranate
Bananas	Cranberries	Raspberries
Blackberries	Oranges	Tomatoes

Superfood Leafy Greens

Too much of any ingredient can alter the taste of a juice drastically. Lucky for you, I have carefully measured and combined leafy greens with ingredients like cucumber, citrus, and apple to neutralize their earthy, peppery flavors. When juiced, leafy greens rank high in vitamins and minerals and energy-giving, brain-powered superfood. The juices made with leafy greens taste great, make you feel great, and provide a sneaky way to get more highly nutritious greens into your diet. Here are some superfood leafy greens included in this book:

Arugula	Chard	Romaine lettuce
Bok choy	Collard greens	Spinach
Cabbage	Kale	

Superfood Vegetables

Balancing the flavor of a juice with a variety of ingredients is where the magic is. Superfood vegetables such as broccoli, butternut squash, and parsnips aren't always thought of as juicing ingredients. Adding superfood vegetables to your juice gives a sense of grounding, uses good detox and cleansing ingredients, and adds tasty, unique flavors to an otherwise average-tasting juice. The other advantage of superfood vegetables is their high nutritional content, such as protein, vitamin C, and calcium, in their raw state. Here are some of the superfood vegetables highlighted in our recipes:

Avocado	Broccoli	Cauliflower
Beet	Butternut squash	Parsnips
Bell pepper		

Superfood Nuts and Seeds

Nuts and seeds provide a significant amount of protein when added to superfood juices. They are also high in healthy monounsaturated and polyunsaturated fats and are rich in B vitamins. They are good choices for pre- and post-workout drinks and are energizing and motivating for a busy workday. The rich, nutty flavors make a delicious, healthy, superfood drink. Here are some of my favorite superfood nuts and seeds:

Almonds	Pistachios
Pecans	Pumpkin seeds

Superfood Spices and Mix-Ins

It's fun to experiment and make new juice recipes with just a few small ingredient mix-ins. Low-calorie, low-sugar superfood spices such as cinnamon and cacao powder can change the taste of a juice with just a teaspoon. Other mix-ins, like chia seeds and flaxseed, can add more fiber to your diet and encourage healthy digestion. Powdered superfood spices and mix-ins are stirred into your superfood juice after everything else has been liquified. Here are some superfood spices and mix-ins you will see in some recipes:

Chia seeds

Cinnamon

Cocoa/cacao

Flaxseed

Ginger

Oats

Spirulina

Turmeric

Mixing Superfoods

Combining superfoods will boost the nutritional value and enhance and change the taste of your juices. You don't need to add every single superfood into every juice to get the benefits. Here are a few stellar superfood combinations:

SUPERFOODS	JUICE BOOST	AMOUNT PER SERVING
Acai + pomegranate	Vitamin C and immunity booster	3½ ounces acai 1 pomegranate
Avocado + spinach	Boosts detoxing and cleansing properties	½ avocado 2 cups spinach
Cabbage + apple	Boosts beneficial bacteria in the gut and creates a sweeter, earthy juice	2 cups shredded cabbage 1 apple
Cacao + cinnamon	Healthy digestion with a sweet-spicy flavor	1 teaspoon ground cacao 1 teaspoon ground cinnamon
Carrots + collard greens	High in beta-carotene that converts to vitamin A for a boost of energy	4 carrots 3 collard green leaves
Chia seeds + lemon	Natural weight loss, liquid energy	2 cups water + juice of ½ lemon 1 tablespoon chia seeds
Coconut water + blueberries	Extra hydration with low calories	8 ounces unsweetened unflavored coconut water 1 cup blueberries
Ginger + turmeric	Extra immunity and a spicier juice	½-inch piece fresh ginger ½-inch piece fresh turmeric root
Grapes + blackberries	Higher antioxidant level and a sweeter juice	½ cup seedless grapes ½ cup blackberries
Kale + almonds	Boosts vitamins E and K, high in antioxidants	4 kale leaves ¼ cup almonds
Spinach + lime	Boosts vitamin C and iron absorption together	1 cup spinach ¼ lime with rind
Spirulina + banana	Powerful nutrient-dense combination with extra vitamins, minerals, and protein	½ teaspoon spirulina 1 medium banana

BE A PRODUCE PRO

Good produce makes great tasting juice. Fruits and vegetables that are fresh, at their perfect ripeness, in season, and organic create high-vitality, energizing superfood juices. Buying quality superfoods enhances your awareness and connection to the food you put into your body. As you step up to your healthy lifestyle, you will see all areas of your life moving toward abundance, gratitude, and self-worth. Here are some tips to becoming a produce pro.

When to Buy

Produce must be ripe to juice but not overripe. Stay clear of produce that looks and smells overripe. If produce smells like it's decomposing or decaying, it probably is. Overripe produce tends to have a higher sugar content and leads to discomfort in your tummy and digestive tract. It's best to buy superfoods that are in season and organic to get the maximum amount of nutrients. If you know what juice you want to make, shop in a timely manner; shopping too many days ahead can result in rotten produce.

How to Wash

Washing fruits and vegetables is a priority. Even if you are using organic produce, there could be wax on it if it is being shipped a long distance, or there could be spray drift from a nearby, nonorganic farm that uses pesticides. Lightly rinsing fruits and vegetables under a stream of water will only wash off visible dirt and residue. I recommend using a designated produce scrub brush and washing and rinsing three times with a produce wash product you can get at most grocery stores. (DIY: Combine 10 percent vinegar and 90 percent water.)

What to Do with Pulp

Juicing will result in pulp, but it doesn't have to go to waste. There are numerous ways to repurpose juice pulp. Composting is a great option if you have a garden, plants, a composting machine, or a designated compost pile. The pulp supplies rich, organic "fertilizer" to plants. You can also use the pulp in recipes, like for crackers, dog treats, fruit leather, and soups. Or re-feed the pulp through the juicer to squeeze out any extra juice. Some recipes offer ideas on how to use the pulp.

Finding Superfood Savings

Bulk bins are places you can find big savings on spices, seeds, nuts, cacao powder, and more. Superfood produce on sale can also be bought in bulk for freezing. I recommend washing, preparing (peeling, cubing, removing pits), and freezing in 1- to 2-cup amounts in labeled freezer bags for 6 to 9 months. To defrost frozen produce, take the desired amount out of the freezer the night before and put it in a large bowl in the refrigerator. For faster thawing, run cold water over your freezer bag, or place the bag in a large bowl full of cold water on your kitchen counter.

SUPER JUICES FAQ

Should I drink from or store juice in plastic containers? Glass or stainless-steel containers are your best bet, as polyurethane will leak into juices from plastic. If plastic containers are stained or scratched, they are leaching. When drinking a super-food with citrus, the acid content will cause the polyurethane to leach, and your juice can possibly become more toxic than good for you. When taking your juice on the go in a stainless-steel tumbler, look for food-grade, BPA-free models. Not only are stainless-steel containers chemical free, but they are also rust-, corrosion-, and stain-resistant, and they don't give mold and bacteria a place to hide.

Can I add ice to my superfood juice? When you add ice to your juice, you dilute the strength of your superfoods. According to traditional Chinese medicine (TCM) practices, putting cold fluids into the stomach weakens the digestive system and creates a chemical imbalance in the body. Ice cubes in a centrifugal juicer will dull the blades, and they soon won't work properly. In a slow masticating juicer, ice cubes will jam the machine, and the auger will wear out. If you want a cooler juice, place your glass in the freezer a few hours before making your juice.

Can a green superfood juice be too green? Leafy greens add iron and fiber to your beverage, but too much can make it bitter and nearly undrinkable. Adding a few extra kale leaves, a few more broccoli florets, or an extra teaspoon of spirulina will definitely give your juice a deeper green color, but an overabundance of green ingredients can irritate your stomach or stomach lining, give you unwanted detoxification symptoms, and cause bloating. The recipes in this book have been carefully tested with the right amount of green ingredients for a happy, healthy tummy.

Is juicing expensive? That depends; if you are starting or sustaining a healthy, balanced lifestyle focused on your well-being, then no. If you are investing in a juicer, buying organic produce, juicing one or two times, and then quitting, then yes. If you have a garden and grow a lot of the produce you use in your juices, that is a wonderful savings. Growing your own produce, taking advantage of sales, and consistently juicing will be less expensive than buying your juices daily. When you commit to juicing, there is no price tag.

Is juicing a fad? For ages, health practitioners have mashed, grated, or ground fresh herbs, vegetables, and soft fruits to make juice. In the 1930s, Dr. Norman Walker invented the first juicing machine, the Norwalk, which is still used today. But the very first mention of attempting to make juice is from the Dead Sea Scrolls, where it has been revealed that mashing pomegranate and figs to make vital juices from fruits and vegetables was recorded before 150 BCE. This primitive mortar-and-pestle process was practiced for profound strength and healing benefits, which we still benefit from today.

ABOUT THE RECIPES

This book is packed with superfood juice recipes to help you feel your best. In addition to the chapter breakdowns by specific health goals, each recipe has two or more of these helpful labels:

- Anti-Inflammatory
- Bone Health
- Brain Boost
- Cleanse and Detox
- Digestive Health
- Heart Health
- Kid Friendly
- Skin Clarity

Each juice includes an explanation of the health benefits, its taste, and the positive characteristics that can affect you—from healing energy to a healthy glow to an extra zing in your day. Some recipes also include these helpful tips:

- Health Tip
- Ingredient Tip
- Preparation Tip
- Substitution Tip
- Troubleshooting Tip

Whether you are looking for an energizing green juice, an eye-opening morning juice, or a sweet immunity booster, I am confident *Superfood Juicing* has plenty of recipes to support you on your health journey.

**Berry Beet Juice
Blend, page 31**

CHAPTER 2

MAGIC MORNING

Raspberry and Spinach Morning Toddy

BONE HEALTH   DIGESTIVE HEALTH   SKIN CLARITY

SERVES 2 • **PREP TIME:** 15 minutes

Spinach is a nutrient superstar, but it's the bright, tart raspberry flavor that dominates this juice. Packed with vitamins A, C, and K, this is an extra-hydrating breakfast juice. Adding a little of the raspberry pulp to the juice provides flavor, fiber, and a feeling of rejuvenation.

2 cups raspberries

2 cups packed shredded iceberg lettuce

2 cups packed baby spinach

2 celery stalks with leaves

1. Feed the raspberries through the juicer.

2. Turn off the juicer and scoop 1 tablespoon of pulp from the pulp basket and set aside.

3. Rotate the lettuce, spinach, and celery through the juicer.

4. Stir the reserved raspberry pulp into the juice, and then drink immediately, or refrigerate in an airtight container for up to 2 days.

PER SERVING (12 TO 16 OUNCES): Calories: 57; Fat: 1g; Protein: 3g; Carbohydrates: 9g; Fiber: 0.5g; Sugar: 7.5g; Sodium: 84mg

Sunshine Spinach Juice

SERVES 2 • **PREP TIME:** 15 minutes

This juice is aptly named because it will leave you feeling sunny and bright, ready to face the day. Apples provide a quick source of energy because they are high in natural sugars. Apples happen to be a member of the rose family, so breathe in their heady sweet fragrance when you cut them.

2 cups packed spinach

2 celery stalks with leaves

2 carrots

2 apples, cored

1 (1-inch) piece fresh
ginger

½ lemon, peeled, seeded,
and sectioned

Rotate the spinach, celery, carrots, apple, ginger, and lemon through the juicer. Drink immediately, or refrigerate in an airtight container for up to 2 days.

INGREDIENT TIP: Pectin, which is found in the plant cells of apples, helps movement through your digestive tract and can help treat digestive disorders.

PER SERVING (12 TO 16 OUNCES): Calories: 120; Fat: 0.5g; Protein: 2g; Carbohydrates: 27g; Fiber: 0g; Sugar: 23g; Sodium: 98mg

Apple, Beet, and Mint Juice

CLEANSE AND DETOX   DIGESTIVE HEALTH   HEART HEALTH

SERVES 2 • **PREP TIME:** 10 minutes

One benefit of drinking juice for breakfast is that it is easier on your digestive system than whole foods—your body absorbs the nutrients more quickly, so you feel the benefits all morning long. The fresh mint in this juice delivers an intoxicating, fresh aroma to help start your day with a calm digestive system.

5 carrots

2 apples, cored

1 small golden beet, chopped

½ cup fresh mint leaves

Rotate the carrots, apples, beet, and mint through the juicer. Drink immediately, or refrigerate in an airtight container for up to 2 days.

PER SERVING (12 TO 16 OUNCES): Calories: 153; Fat: 1g; Protein: 3g; Carbohydrates: 33g; Fiber: 0g; Sugar: 28g; Sodium: 138mg

Blueberry Walnut Juice

BRAIN BOOST   HEART HEALTH   KID FRIENDLY

SERVES 1 • **PREP TIME:** 15 minutes

Raw nuts and seeds are rich in protein and heart-healthy fats. This recipe uses walnuts for a rich, nutty flavor. Try to find black walnuts, which don't have the bitter taste sometimes associated with other types of walnuts. This sweet, nutty juice will give you extra energy and focus to start your day.

1 cup blueberries
1 apple, cored
½ cup packed baby
  spinach
½ lemon with rind, seeded
¼ cup raw walnuts

1. Rotate the blueberries, apple, spinach, and lemon through the juicer.

2. In a blender, combine the juice and walnuts. Blend on high speed for 30 seconds, or until smooth. Drink immediately, or refrigerate in an airtight container for up to 24 hours.

PER SERVING (14 TO 18 OUNCES): Calories: 345; Fat: 17g; Protein: 6g; Carbohydrates: 42g; Fiber: 1.5g; Sugar: 35g; Sodium: 25mg

Brilliant Blueberry Breakfast Blend

BRAIN BOOST   HEART HEALTH   SKIN CLARITY

SERVES 1 • **PREP TIME:** 15 minutes

This recipe is designed to wake you up with a burst of flavor and natural energy. The high amount of vitamin C in kiwi and blueberries will boost your immune system to give you a healthy start to your day.

1 cup blueberries
2 kiwis, peeled
6 romaine lettuce leaves
1 dill sprig

Rotate the blueberries, kiwis, lettuce, and dill through the juicer. Drink immediately, or refrigerate in an airtight container for up to 24 hours.

PER SERVING (12 TO 16 OUNCES): Calories: 169; Fat: 1.5g; Protein: 4g; Carbohydrates: 35g; Fiber: 0g; Sugar: 28g; Sodium: 30mg

Blueberry Banana Booster

HEART HEALTH   KID FRIENDLY   SKIN CLARITY

SERVES 1 • **PREP TIME:** 10 minutes

The combination of blueberries and bananas is a classic favorite. Adding cucumber and carrot inspires a refreshing, slightly sweet, grounding good morning juice. Bananas and blueberries are both rich in antioxidants and potassium, which help keep skin looking youthful.

2 cups blueberries
1 large carrot
½ cucumber, peeled and halved lengthwise
1 medium banana, peeled

1. Rotate the blueberries, carrot, and cucumber through the juicer.

2. In a blender, combine the juice and banana. Blend on high speed for 30 seconds, or until smooth. Drink immediately, or refrigerate in an airtight container for up to 24 hours.

PER SERVING (16 TO 20 OUNCES): Calories: 289; Fat: 1.5g; Protein: 4g; Carbohydrates: 65g; Fiber: 3g; Sugar: 48g; Sodium: 48mg

Cucumber Apple Kale Juice

CLEANSE AND DETOX   DIGESTIVE HEALTH   SKIN CLARITY

SERVES 1 • **PREP TIME:** 15 minutes

Cucumber is known for its high water content and detoxifying qualities. Apples, on the other hand, are known for their high concentration of phytonutrients, which help regulate blood sugar levels—a benefit particularly valuable for diabetics. This juice provides clear thinking for a productive day.

1 large English cucumber, peeled and halved lengthwise

2 medium Golden Delicious apples, cored

2 large curly kale leaves, deveined

Rotate the cucumber, apples, and kale through the juicer. Drink immediately, or refrigerate in an airtight container for up to 24 hours.

SUBSTITUTION TIP: You can substitute a Fuji apple for a Golden Delicious for a slightly sweeter, more robust juice.

PER SERVING (14 TO 18 OUNCES): Calories: 217; Fat: 1g; Protein: 7g; Carbohydrates: 45g; Fiber: 0g; Sugar: 39g; Sodium: 39mg

Berry Beet Juice Blend

CLEANSE AND DETOX   DIGESTIVE HEALTH   HEART HEALTH

SERVES 2 • **PREP TIME:** 10 minutes

Beets have been shown to enhance exercise performance because they contain nutrients that oxygenate the blood, improving recovery time. In this recipe, the oxygen-boosting power of beets combines beautifully with the sweet flavor and antioxidant power of fresh blackberries. This earthy, fruity juice is the perfect balance to keep you grounded all day.

2 medium beets, including
  greens
1 cup blackberries
1 large carrot
1 medium pear, cored

Rotate the beets and greens, blackberries, carrot, and pear through the juicer. Drink immediately, or refrigerate in an airtight container for up to 2 days.

PER SERVING (10 TO 14 OUNCES): Calories: 108; Fat: 0.5g; Protein: 4g; Carbohydrates: 22g; Fiber: 0g; Sugar: 19g; Sodium: 183mg

Seize the Day

ANTI-INFLAMMATORY   DIGESTIVE HEALTH   HEART HEALTH

SERVES 1 • **PREP TIME:** 20 minutes

Can't decide between green juice, green tea, or a morning fiber drink? Why not choose them all? Spinach provides antioxidants, green tea gives you energy, and flaxseed supports a healthy digestive tract. The texture is a bit thick due to the ground flaxseed, but the taste is delicious. Your clear, flowing digestive tract will provide you with a happy, focused mind.

2 cups packed baby spinach

1 red apple, cored

¾ cup brewed green tea, cooled

2 teaspoons ground flaxseed

1. Rotate the spinach and apple through the juicer.

2. Stir in the green tea and flaxseed thoroughly and drink immediately.

HEALTH TIP: Because flaxseed contains a high amount of oil, ground flaxseed can spoil quickly—in as little as a week. It's best to buy whole seeds and use a clean spice or coffee grinder to grind only what you need.

PER SERVING (16 OUNCES): Calories: 146; Fat: 2g; Protein: 5g; Carbohydrates: 27g; Fiber: 1g; Sugar: 22g; Sodium: 91mg

Make My Day Juice

BONE HEALTH   **HEART HEALTH**   **SKIN CLARITY**

SERVES 2 • **PREP TIME:** 15 minutes

This sweet, refreshing juice will make your day. The mint stimulates your mind, the kale detoxifies your body, and the oranges and carrots keep you looking and feeling vibrant. Drinking this nutrient-rich juice first thing in the morning on an empty stomach is the best way to absorb more nutrients quickly.

5 carrots

2 oranges, peeled, seeded, and sectioned

½ lemon, peeled and seeded

8 kale leaves, deveined

15 fresh mint leaves

Rotate the carrots, oranges, lemon, kale, and mint through the juicer. Drink immediately, or refrigerate in an airtight container for up to 2 days.

| **SUBSTITUTION TIP:** Perk up the flavor with fresh rosemary instead of mint.

PER SERVING (12 TO 16 OUNCES): Calories: 156; Fat: 0.5g; Protein: 6g; Carbohydrates: 32g; Fiber: 0g; Sugar: 20g; Sodium: 153mg

Down-to-Earth Juice

SERVES 2 • **PREP TIME:** 15 minutes

The best word to describe cabbage juice is "earthy." Cabbage is great for diges-tion and can increase the beneficial bacteria in the gut. The apples add a sweetness you'll appreciate as you optimize your greens and vegetables for a healthy day.

½ cup packed shredded
   green cabbage
3 celery stalks
1 cucumber, peeled and
   halved lengthwise
1 cup packed baby
   spinach
2 apples, cored

Rotate the cabbage, celery, cucumber, spinach, and apples through the juicer. Drink immediately, or refrigerate in an airtight container for up to 24 hours.

INGREDIENT TIP: Cabbage is a great source of vitamin K_1, providing 85 percent of your daily recommendation in just 1 cup.

PER SERVING (12 TO 18 OUNCES): Calories: 108; Fat: 0.5g; Protein: 2g; Carbohydrates: 24g; Fiber: 0g; Sugar: 21g; Sodium: 77mg

Heavenly Delight

BONE HEALTH   **BRAIN BOOST**   KID FRIENDLY

SERVES 1 • **PREP TIME:** 10 minutes

Raspberries, coconut, and chocolate are a match made in heaven, and I was thrilled to find a way to use all three in a green juice recipe. Raw cacao, which is the purest form of chocolate, is a low-sugar, low-calorie ingredient that promotes weight loss and boosts immunity—a wonderful health-conscious way to have morning chocolate!

½ cup raspberries

4 kale leaves, deveined

½ red apple, cored

1 cup unsweetened unflavored coconut water

1 tablespoon raw cacao powder

1. Rotate the raspberries, kale, and apple through the juicer.

2. Stir in the coconut water and cacao powder. Drink immediately, or refrigerate in an airtight container for up to 24 hours.

HEALTH TIP: Cacao and cocoa are both from the same plant. Raw cacao powder, however, is made by cold pressing unroasted cacao beans, and it contains living enzymes. Cocoa powder is raw cacao that's been roasted.

PER SERVING (16 OUNCES): Calories: 209; Fat: 1g; Protein: 6g; Carbohydrates: 44g; Fiber: 2g; Sugar: 31g; Sodium: 113mg

Fine Line Wine

SERVES 2 • **PREP TIME:** 10 minutes

Starting your day with this berry-packed recipe is an awesome choice for breakfast. The five different berries (grapes are botanically considered a berry) contain a high amount of vitamin C, which helps fight inflammation and strengthens the immune system. Have a berry sweet day!

2 apples, cored
½ cup blueberries
½ cup blackberries
½ cup raspberries
½ cup strawberries
½ cup seedless red grapes

Rotate the apples, blueberries, blackberries, raspberries, strawberries, and grapes through the juicer. Drink immediately, or refrigerate in an airtight container for up to 24 hours.

HEALTH TIP: Berries are full of antioxidants that fight cancer and disease. In addition to their fabulous vitamins and mineral content, they also have brain-boosting omega-3s.

PER SERVING (10 TO 14 OUNCES): Calories: 217; Fat: 1g; Protein: 2g; Carbohydrates: 50g; Fiber: 0g; Sugar: 43g; Sodium: 3mg

Blueberry Cabbage Juice

BRAIN BOOST DIGESTIVE HEALTH **HEART HEALTH**

SERVES 1 • **PREP TIME:** 20 minutes

If you like to start your morning with something sweet, skip the toaster pastries and go for this juice. The red cabbage is rich in antioxidants and vitamins A, C, and K that help protect against cellular damage. Not only is this juice packed with vitamins and minerals, but it is also sweet, colorful, and uplifting to boot.

1 cup blueberries

1 cucumber, peeled and halved lengthwise

1 apple, cored

1 cup packed shredded red cabbage

Rotate the blueberries, cucumber, apple, and cabbage through the juicer. Drink immediately, or refrigerate in an airtight container for up to 24 hours.

INGREDIENT TIP: Blueberries are a superfood full of antioxidants and vitamins B_2, C, and E. They can reduce the risk of developing Alzheimer's disease. Try all the different types of blueberries, including wild blueberries if they are available in your area.

PER SERVING (16 TO 20 OUNCES): Calories: 205; Fat: 1g; Protein: 4g; Carbohydrates: 45g; Fiber: 0g; Sugar: 39g; Sodium: 26mg

Sweet Romaine Apple Juice

CLEANSE AND DETOX   DIGESTIVE HEALTH   HEART HEALTH

SERVES 3 • **PREP TIME:** 20 minutes

Many people have a hard time sticking to their juice routine because they get bored with the recipes or find the strong taste unpleasant. Although this recipe is made with romaine lettuce, all you will taste is the sweetness of apples. This juice is a great choice for beginner juicer enthusiasts who are becoming familiar with the juicing process. Enjoy drinking this cheerful, energy-filled superfood juice.

4 cups packed shredded romaine lettuce

4 apples, cored

Rotate the lettuce and apples through the juicer. Drink immediately, or refrigerate in an airtight container for up to 24 hours.

INGREDIENT TIP: Romaine lettuce is a common ingredient in many kitchens, but you might not realize it is also very nutritious—an excellent source of vitamins A, C, B_1, and B_2. Make sure you wash every leaf individually because grit and dirt can hide between the leaves.

PER SERVING (12 TO 14 OUNCES): Calories: 120; Fat: 0.5g; Protein: 1g; Carbohydrates: 28g; Fiber: 0g; Sugar: 26g; Sodium: 7mg

Clear and Clean Juice Blend

BONE HEALTH   CLEANSE AND DETOX   DIGESTIVE HEALTH

SERVES 2 • **PREP TIME:** 15 minutes

A sluggish digestive tract can mean a sluggish mind. Combining juicing diges-tive aids, like apples and beets, with spirulina protein and high-fiber flaxseed encourages a clear body and mind. Drink this juice first thing in the morning for confidence in your mind and body for a productive day.

2 Granny Smith apples, cored

1 small golden beet

2 cups packed baby spinach

1 teaspoon spirulina powder

1 teaspoon ground flaxseed

1 frozen banana, peeled

1. Rotate the apples, beet, and spinach through the juicer.

2. In a blender, combine the juice, spirulina, flaxseed, and banana. Blend on high speed for 30 seconds, or until smooth. Drink immediately.

HEALTH TIP: Spirulina is a blue-green algae with powerful antioxidant and anti-inflammatory properties. It's loaded with various nutrients, such as vitamins B_1, B_2, and B_3; copper; iron; and protein. Stay true to the amount of spirulina powder in this recipe, as the taste can become overwhelming if overdone.

PER SERVING (12 TO 16 OUNCES): Calories: 161; Fat: 1g; Protein: 4g; Carbohydrates: 34g; Fiber: 2g; Sugar: 26g; Sodium: 95mg

Hawaiian Sunrise Juice

BRAIN BOOST   KID FRIENDLY   SKIN CLARITY

SERVES 1 • **PREP TIME:** 15 minutes

Do you have a morning meeting or exercise class or just want an extra energy boost? The ginger adds an extra-spicy kick to this pineapple, spinach, and lime juice. The high vitamin C content in the pineapple and lime will boost your immunity, give you energy, and sweeten your day.

2 cups cubed pineapple

2 cups packed baby spinach

1 (½-inch) piece fresh ginger

½ lime with the rind, seeded and sectioned

Rotate the pineapple, spinach, ginger, and lime through the juicer. Drink immediately, or refrigerate in an airtight container for up to 2 days.

SUBSTITUTION TIP: If you don't have a lime, use half a lemon; remember to keep the rind on for those extra vitamins and minerals. Lemons are usually larger than limes, so you'll get an extra boost of vitamin C.

PER SERVING (18 TO 22 OUNCES): Calories: 192; Fat: 0.5g; Protein: 4g; Carbohydrates: 43g; Fiber: 0g; Sugar: 32g; Sodium: 90mg

Vegetable 8

BONE HEALTH   DIGESTIVE HEALTH   HEART HEALTH

SERVES 2 • **PREP TIME:** 15 minutes

This healthier version of the classic store-bought juice contains no additives and provides an array of vitamins and minerals. Vitamin A boosts your immune system, and vitamin C assists with bone health and injury repair. Potassium helps regulate blood pressure and muscle growth. Robust in flavor and texture, this drink will fill you up and keep you going for hours.

2 medium tomatoes

1 cucumber, peeled and halved lengthwise

1 cup packed baby spinach

1 cup shredded green cabbage

½ red bell pepper, seeded and sectioned

2 celery stalks

2 carrots

1 scallion, white and green parts

Rotate the tomatoes, cucumber, spinach, cabbage, bell pepper, celery, carrots, and scallion through the juicer. Drink immediately, or refrigerate in an airtight container for up to 24 hours.

INGREDIENT TIP: How many vegetables does it take to make 1 cup of juice? One English cucumber will yield 1 cup of juice, as will 9 medium carrots, 1 bunch of celery, or 3 medium tomatoes.

PER SERVING (12 TO 16 OUNCES): Calories: 68; Fat: 0.5g; Protein: 4g; Carbohydrates: 12g; Fiber: 0g; Sugar: 10g; Sodium: 114mg

Spinach, Cucumber, and Minty Beet Juice

CLEANSE AND DETOX   DIGESTIVE HEALTH   HEART HEALTH

SERVES 1 • **PREP TIME:** 15 minutes

Beets are a rich source of antioxidants, and they are anti-inflammatory. They are also high in folate and contain copper, iron, magnesium, manganese, and phosphorus. The particular makeup of beet fiber makes it especially adept at fighting colon cancer and cardiovascular disease. As beets are very sweet, it takes only a small amount to add plenty of flavor.

½ beet with leaves (leaves optional)

2 cups packed baby spinach

1 tablespoon fresh mint leaves

2 cucumbers, peeled and halved lengthwise

1. Feed the beet and beet leaves (if using) through the juicer.

2. Turn off the juicer and scoop 1 tablespoon of pulp from the pulp basket. Set aside.

3. Rotate the spinach, mint, and cucumbers through the juicer.

4. Stir the reserved beet pulp into the juice, and then drink immediately.

PER SERVING (18 TO 22 OUNCES): Calories: 68; Fat: 0.5g; Protein: 6g; Carbohydrates: 10g; Fiber: 0.5g; Sugar: 8.5g; Sodium: 128mg

Spinach Almond Juice

BONE HEALTH · **BRAIN BOOST** · HEART HEALTH

SERVES 1 • **PREP TIME:** 10 minutes

Almonds are an excellent source of protein, magnesium, and calcium—three nutrients that help keep energy flowing in your body and are key to bone health. Almonds also contain riboflavin, which helps support aerobic energy production. Protein from the spinach and almonds will keep you energized and alert throughout your morning.

½ cup packed baby spinach
1 celery stalk with leaves
1 apple, cored
¼ cup raw almonds

1. Rotate the spinach, celery, and apple through the juicer.

2. In a blender, combine the juice and the almonds. Blend on high speed for 30 seconds, or until smooth. Drink immediately.

| **TROUBLESHOOTING TIP:** If the juice is too thick, stir in ¼ cup of water to thin it.

PER SERVING (12 TO 16 OUNCES): Calories: 387; Fat: 27g; Protein: 9g; Carbohydrates: 27g; Fiber: 5.5g; Sugar: 19g; Sodium: 62mg

Orange Energy Healer,
page 56

ENERGY SURGE

Apple, Pecan, and Cinnamon Juice

BRAIN BOOST   CLEANSE AND DETOX   KID FRIENDLY

SERVES 2 • **PREP TIME:** 10 minutes

In addition to being full of flavor, pecans are also a great source of antioxidants and zinc, which benefit brain function and cell growth. In this recipe, they are flavored with a hint of cinnamon. This juice is like apple crumble in a glass.

2 green apples, cored
1 cucumber, peeled and
   halved lengthwise
1 celery stalk with leaves
1 romaine lettuce leaf
¼ cup raw pecans
¼ teaspoon ground
   cinnamon

1. Rotate the apples, cucumber, celery, and lettuce through the juicer.

2. In a blender, combine the juice, pecans, and cinnamon. Blend on high speed for 30 seconds, or until smooth. Drink immediately, or refrigerate in an airtight container for up to 24 hours.

HEALTH TIP: This sweet treat is a great recipe to get kids juicing; they can help you juice and blend!

PER SERVING (12 TO 16 OUNCES): Calories: 177; Fat: 9.5g; Protein: 3g; Carbohydrates: 20g; Fiber: 1.5g; Sugar: 18g; Sodium: 22mg

Refreshing Red Berry Juice

SERVES 2 • **PREP TIME:** 10 minutes

Berries are an excellent source of vitamins and minerals, including vitamin C, calcium, iron, and potassium, and they have high antioxidant levels and anti-inflammatory properties. Feel the abundant, natural energy from this potent juice.

2 cups strawberries

1 cup raspberries

1 cup gooseberries

1 cup seedless red grapes

Rotate the strawberries, raspberries, gooseberries, and grapes through the juicer. Drink immediately, or refrigerate in an airtight container for up to 2 days.

SUBSTITUTION TIP: If you can't find fresh gooseberries at your local health food store or farmers' market, substitute yellow cherry tomatoes. They both have the sweet-tart quality that works well with this recipe.

PER SERVING (12 TO 16 OUNCES): Calories: 141; Fat: 1g; Protein: 3g; Carbohydrates: 30g; Fiber: 0g; Sugar: 22g; Sodium: 3mg

Raspberry Spinach Refresher

BONE HEALTH | **BRAIN BOOST** | **HEART HEALTH**

SERVES 1 • **PREP TIME:** 15 minutes

Everything about this recipe is refreshing—from the crisp flavor of spinach to the sweetness of raspberries and the coolness of cilantro. Sip on a hot day, after a workout, or as an afternoon midday juice snack.

2 cups raspberries

1 bunch baby spinach, or
   2 cups packed

1 small lime, peeled,
   seeded, and sectioned

2 or 3 cilantro sprigs

Rotate the raspberries, spinach, lime, and cilantro through the juicer. Drink immediately, or refrigerate in an airtight container for up to 2 days.

PER SERVING (12 TO 16 OUNCES): Calories: 109; Fat: 1.5g; Protein: 6g; Carbohydrates: 18g; Fiber: 0g; Sugar: 11g; Sodium: 94mg

Daily Endurance Juice

BONE HEALTH   **HEART HEALTH**   SKIN CLARITY

SERVES 1 • **PREP TIME:** 15 minutes

Broccoli packs a punch in this juice that has nearly 270 percent of your daily vitamin C requirement. Broccoli also contains about 3 grams of protein per cup. Many athletes choose broccoli because it contains the nutrients needed to enhance tissue growth and heal the body.

2 cups broccoli florets

2 cucumbers, peeled and halved lengthwise

1 Granny Smith apple, cored

2 mint sprigs

Rotate the broccoli, cucumbers, apple, and mint through the juicer. Drink immediately, or refrigerate in an airtight container for up to 2 days.

HEALTH TIP: Don't throw out those broccoli stems. Their nutritional value is nearly identical to that of the florets, and they taste even sweeter. The stems can be juiced or used in other recipes like broccoli stem pesto.

PER SERVING (18 TO 22 OUNCES): Calories: 153; Fat: 1.5g; Protein: 7g; Carbohydrates: 28g; Fiber: 0g; Sugar: 24g; Sodium: 49mg

Motivate Me

SERVES 1 • **PREP TIME:** 15 minutes

Thick and dark green, this unusual-looking juice tastes like a blueberry dessert, only it's much healthier. Maca reportedly helps you gain muscle, increases strength, boosts energy, and improves physical performance. Motivation? Check!

1 cup blueberries

2 cups packed baby spinach

1 cucumber, peeled and halved lengthwise

1 (½-inch) piece fresh ginger

½ teaspoon maca powder

½ teaspoon ground cinnamon

1. Rotate the blueberries, spinach, cucumber, and ginger through the juicer.

2. Stir in the maca powder and cinnamon, and then drink immediately.

INGREDIENT TIP: A cinnamon tree can grow up to 60 feet tall. The spice you eat comes from the bark.

PER SERVING (14 TO 18 OUNCES): Calories: 121; Fat: 1g; Protein: 5g; Carbohydrates: 23g; Fiber: 1g; Sugar: 18g; Sodium: 92mg

Looking Good, Feeling Good

CLEANSE AND DETOX   HEART HEALTH   SKIN CLARITY

SERVES 1 • **PREP TIME:** 10 minutes

This juice is an all-around tonic that benefits your whole body and helps you shed weight more easily. Tomatoes, a good source of the antioxidant lycopene, help reduce the risk of heart disease and cancer. Carrots are beneficial for healthy, vibrant skin, and beets assist the liver in detoxifying the body. This juice's gentle cleansing properties bring a balance of energy and calm.

---

1 bunch beet greens (5 or 6 stems)

1 green apple, cored

1 cucumber, peeled and halved lengthwise

2 carrots

1 tomato

1 (½-inch) piece fresh ginger

Rotate the beet greens, apple, cucumber, carrots, tomato, and ginger through the juicer. Drink immediately, or refrigerate in an airtight container for up to 2 days.

HEALTH TIP: You can juice the green tops of beets and even put them in salads. The oxalic acid in these greens can be harmful when consumed in large amounts, but in small amounts, they are perfectly fine. Consult your doctor if you are concerned.

PER SERVING (16 TO 20 OUNCES): Calories: 189; Fat: 1.5g; Protein: 10g; Carbohydrates: 34g; Fiber: 0g; Sugar: 29g; Sodium: 673mg

Electrolyte Power Juice

BONE HEALTH   DIGESTIVE HEALTH   **HEART HEALTH**

SERVES 2 • **PREP TIME:** 10 minutes

Electrolytes are necessary for proper functioning of the cardiac, digestive, muscular, and nervous systems. Electrolytes contain calcium, magnesium, potassium, and sodium to hydrate your cells so everything runs smoothly. Skip the premade electrolyte drinks that contain added sugar and go with this fresh green juice instead.

2 cups packed baby spinach

6 celery stalks

1 cup blueberries

8 ounces unsweetened unflavored coconut water

1. Rotate the spinach, celery, and blueberries through the juicer.

2. Stir in the coconut water, and then drink immediately.

SUBSTITUTION TIP: To try a variety of flavors, swap the blueberries for strawberries, cherries, or watermelon. Berries are high in vitamins A and C, making them great for heart health. Watermelon contains thiamine, folate, and vitamin B_6, all of which boost energy.

PER SERVING (16 TO 20 OUNCES): Calories: 80; Fat: 0.5g; Protein: 3g; Carbohydrates: 16g; Fiber: 0g; Sugar: 13g; Sodium: 170mg

Juice of Champions

SERVES 1 • **PREP TIME:** 15 minutes

This hearty juice is both flavorful and good for your heart. Beets contain high levels of antioxidants and other vitamins that help lower blood pressure, boost endurance, and fight cancer. Beets also help boost immunity. This juice is a wonderful pre- or post-workout drink.

1 cucumber, peeled and halved lengthwise

1 Swiss chard leaf, deveined

2 cilantro sprigs

½ small to medium golden or red beet

3 celery stalks

½ lemon, peeled, seeded, and sectioned

1 (½-inch) piece fresh ginger

Rotate the cucumber, chard, cilantro, beet, celery, lemon, and ginger through the juicer. Drink immediately, or refrigerate in an airtight container for up to 24 hours.

HEALTH TIP: Many heart-shaped fruits and vegetables are truly good for your heart. That's another good reason to consider choosing apples, beets, strawberries, and tomatoes the next time you buy fruits and vegetables.

PER SERVING (16 OUNCES): Calories: 60; Fat: 0.5g; Protein: 4g; Carbohydrates: 10g; Fiber: 0g; Sugar: 8.5g; Sodium: 239mg

Cherry Berry Blast

ANTI-INFLAMMATORY   KID FRIENDLY   SKIN CLARITY

SERVES 1 • **PREP TIME:** 15 minutes

Dark berries, like blackberries, tend to be higher in antioxidants than lighter-colored ones, which may reduce inflammation and fatigue, providing the body with energy and vitality. The hint of cinnamon adds anti-inflammatory properties, more antioxidants, and an energizing spice that might trick you into thinking you are having berry pie.

2 cups cherries, pitted
1 cup strawberries
1 cup blackberries
Pinch ground cinnamon

1. Rotate the cherries, strawberries, and blackberries through the juicer.

2. Stir in the cinnamon, and then drink immediately, or refrigerate in an airtight container for up to 2 days.

HEALTH TIP: Try blending this berry pulp into your next smoothie. It will add extra flavor, texture, and nutrients to your drink. The pulp can be refrigerated in an airtight container for up to 2 days.

PER SERVING (18 TO 22 OUNCES): Calories: 269; Fat: 1.5g; Protein: 6g; Carbohydrates: 58g; Fiber: 0g; Sugar: 53g; Sodium: 3mg

Blueberry Broccoli Juice

ANTI-INFLAMMATORY   BONE HEALTH   DIGESTIVE HEALTH

SERVES 1 • **PREP TIME:** 10 minutes

Broccoli is packed with vitamin K, which your body needs to help absorb calcium, which is important to maintaining strong bones and teeth. Broccoli, lemon, and blueberries are all high in antioxidants, making this high–vitamin, mineral, antioxidant juice an amazing energy drink.

2 celery stalks with leaves

1 head broccoli, cut into florets and stalks saved for another use

1 cup blueberries

½ lemon, peeled, seeded, and sectioned

Rotate the celery, broccoli, blueberries, and lemon through the juicer. Drink immediately, or refrigerate in an airtight container for up to 24 hours.

PER SERVING (12 TO 16 OUNCES): Calories: 121; Fat: 1g; Protein: 5g; Carbohydrates: 23g; Fiber: 0g; Sugar: 19g; Sodium: 96mg

Orange Energy Healer

ANTI-INFLAMMATORY   **HEART HEALTH**   **KID FRIENDLY**

SERVES 1 • **PREP TIME:** 10 minutes

This ultra-orange juice has a secret ingredient: turmeric root. The main ingredient in turmeric is curcumin, which is a powerful antioxidant and anti- inflammatory. Turmeric's inspiring, uplifting, vibrant orange color gives this root superfood status.

**2 Granny Smith apples,
  cored**

**1 orange, peeled, seeded,
  and sectioned**

2 carrots

**1 (1-inch) piece fresh
  turmeric**

**Dash freshly ground black
  pepper**

1. Rotate the apples, orange, carrots, and turmeric through the juicer.

2. Stir in the black pepper, and then drink immediately, or refrigerate in an airtight container for up to 24 hours.

INGREDIENT TIP: Piperine, found in black pepper, enhances the absorption of the curcumin in turmeric. For a spicier juice, try two dashes of pepper.

PER SERVING (16 TO 20 OUNCES): Calories: 257; Fat: 1.5g; Protein: 4g; Carbohydrates: 57g; Fiber: 0g; Sugar: 50g; Sodium: 88mg

Energy Balance Juice

DIGESTIVE HEALTH KID FRIENDLY SKIN CLARITY

SERVES 1 • **PREP TIME:** 15 minutes

Serotonin, an enzyme present in kiwi fruit, helps steer you away from depression to better balance your mood and alleviate stress. This recipe brings more ease and self-assurance to your day, with a little kick of lemon to bring positive energy.

2 kiwis, peeled

1 Granny Smith apple, cored

1 cucumber, peeled and halved lengthwise

2 cups packed baby spinach

½ lemon with the rind, seeded and sectioned

Rotate the kiwis, apple, cucumber, spinach, and lemon through the juicer. Drink immediately, or refrigerate in an airtight container for up to 24 hours.

HEALTH TIP: The lemon peel and juice both contain vitamin C. By juicing them together, you double your immunity boost.

PER SERVING (16 TO 20 OUNCES): Calories: 197; Fat: 1.5g; Protein: 6g; Carbohydrates: 40g; Fiber: 0g; Sugar: 32g; Sodium: 97mg

Kale, Apple, and Broccoli Juice

BONE HEALTH   DIGESTIVE HEALTH   HEART HEALTH

SERVES 1 • **PREP TIME:** 10 minutes

Kale is not only a great source of natural energy, but it is also loaded with anti-oxidants. You can use any variety of kale in this recipe, including curly, green, purple, or red. This is a good starter juice if you're unsure about juices with kale because the recipe doesn't call for much so the flavor is milder.

2 kale leaves, deveined

2 broccoli stalks, peeled

2 Granny Smith apples, cored

Rotate the kale, broccoli, and apples through the juicer. Drink immediately, or refrigerate in an airtight container for up to 24 hours.

PER SERVING (14 TO 18 OUNCES): Calories: 254; Fat: 2.5g; Protein: 12g; Carbohydrates: 46g; Fiber: 0g; Sugar: 39g; Sodium: 103mg

Cherry Berry Lemonade

BRAIN BOOST **KID FRIENDLY** **SKIN CLARITY**

SERVES 1 • **PREP TIME:** 10 minutes

You can take this juice with you for lunch on the go without worrying about it losing nutrients because the lemon juice slows the oxidation process. This sweet-and-sour tonic is a pick-me-up juice that is packed with vitamins, minerals, and antioxidants.

1 cup sour cherries, pitted
1 cup raspberries
1 cup blueberries
½ lemon with rind, seeded and sectioned

Rotate the cherries, raspberries, blueberries, and lemon through the juicer. Drink immediately, or refrigerate in an airtight container for up to 24 hours.

HEALTH TIP: Use the pulp from this recipe for a yummy tea. Fill a tea ball with the pulp and steep in hot water for 20 minutes. To sweeten your tea, use a natural sweetener, like stevia or agave.

PER SERVING (14 TO 18 OUNCES): Calories: 201; Fat: 1.5g; Protein: 4g; Carbohydrates: 43g; Fiber: 0g; Sugar: 35g; Sodium: 8mg

Pineapple, Cauliflower, and Green Cabbage Blend

BONE HEALTH   DIGESTIVE HEALTH   HEART HEALTH

SERVES 1 • **PREP TIME:** 20 minutes

Juicy, sweet pineapple dominates the flavor of this nutritious juice, which is why the other ingredients are all vegetables that are not sweet. The combination of cauliflower, greens, and pineapple loads you up with vitamins A and C, B vitamins, copper, and manganese. This powerful juice will give you enough energy to run an extra mile, swim a few more laps, or surf a few more waves.

2 cups cauliflower florets

2 cups packed shredded green cabbage

4 romaine lettuce leaves

1 cup cubed pineapple

Rotate the cauliflower, cabbage, lettuce, and pineapple through the juicer. Drink immediately, or refrigerate in an airtight container for up to 24 hours.

PER SERVING (16 TO 20 OUNCES): Calories: 165; Fat: 1g; Protein: 8g; Carbohydrates: 31g; Fiber: 0g; Sugar: 25g; Sodium: 110mg

Tomato Gazpacho Juice

SERVES 1 • **PREP TIME:** 15 minutes

When you think of antioxidants, you probably think of fruit. Tomatoes are also a fruit and are rich in a certain antioxidant called lycopene. Lycopene is actually more abundant when tomatoes are cooked, but they still provide plenty of disease-fighting punch in this recipe in their raw form. Garlic is also incredibly high in antioxidants, so try this juice when you are fighting a cold, are feeling run-down, or just need a boost of energy.

4 plum tomatoes, sectioned

1 green bell pepper, cored and seeded

1 cucumber, peeled and halved lengthwise

1 cup fresh cilantro

1 garlic clove, peeled

Rotate the tomatoes, bell pepper, cucumber, cilantro, and garlic through the juicer. Drink immediately, or refrigerate in an airtight container for up to 24 hours.

| **SUBSTITUTION TIP:** If you want a milder herb or aren't a fan of cilantro, try parsley instead.

PER SERVING (16 TO 20 OUNCES): Calories: 85; Fat: 1g; Protein: 5g; Carbohydrates: 14g; Fiber: 0g; Sugar: 12g; Sodium: 28mg

Apple Arugula Juice

SERVES 1 • **PREP TIME:** 10 minutes

Arugula is a bitter green that helps detoxify the body. When arugula is combined with apples, as in this recipe, the apple's taste dominates. It is best to use sweeter apples in this juice to offset the peppery flavor of the arugula. Try Gala or Honeycrisp varieties rather than McIntosh or Granny Smith. This is a great juice for when you need a late-afternoon pick-me-up.

2 apples, cored
½ cup packed arugula
1 celery stalk with leaves
½ lemon, seeded

Rotate the apples, arugula, celery, and lemon through the juicer. Drink immediately, or refrigerate in an airtight container for up to 24 hours.

INGREDIENT TIP: Arugula, also known as rocket in parts of Europe and Australia, is a pretty green color and has powerful disease-fighting nutrients. It is a great source of vitamin K and folic acid. Arugula can promote a healthy immune system and help prevent cancer and Alzheimer's disease.

PER SERVING (12 TO 16 OUNCES): Calories: 188; Fat: 0.5g; Protein: 2g; Carbohydrates: 44g; Fiber: 0g; Sugar: 40g; Sodium: 42mg

Cherry Coconut Juice

BRAIN BOOST **HEART HEALTH** **KID FRIENDLY**

SERVES 2 • **PREP TIME:** 15 minutes

Coconut water is full of energy-giving electrolytes like potassium, magnesium, and calcium, making this juice a top choice for a post-workout drink. Staying hydrated through coconut's naturally sweet water tastes great, balances the system, and is a great addition to your healthy lifestyle.

---

2 cups cherries, pitted

2 cups unsweetened
   unflavored coconut
   water

1. Feed the cherries through the juicer.

2. Stir in the coconut water, and then drink immediately, or refrigerate in an airtight container for up to 24 hours.

HEALTH TIP: To make cherry fruit leather with the pulp: Line a baking sheet with parchment paper. Press the fruit pulp evenly on the sheet; then place it in a dehydrator set at 108°F or in your oven at its lowest setting (around 115°F) for 12 to 14 hours. Cut into strips and enjoy!

PER SERVING (14 TO 18 OUNCES): Calories: 136; Fat: 0.5g; Protein: 2g; Carbohydrates: 31g; Fiber: 0g; Sugar: 29g; Sodium: 62mg

Collard Greens, Zucchini, and Beet Toddy

BONE HEALTH   DIGESTIVE HEALTH   HEART HEALTH

SERVES 1 • **PREP TIME:** 15 minutes

As with other cruciferous vegetables, collard greens have strong cancer-fighting benefits. Few vegetables can compete with collards for vitamin K abundance, which improves calcium absorption. They also contain plenty of vitamins A and C, iron, and manganese, which help protect the body from free radicals and aid blood sugar stabilization. This health-conscious juice will optimize your daily self-care routine.

---

1 cup packed deveined collard green leaves

2 zucchini, halved lengthwise

½ golden beet

4 celery stalks with leaves

Rotate the collard greens, zucchini, beet, and celery through the juicer. Drink immediately, or refrigerate in an airtight container for up to 24 hours.

PER SERVING (16 TO 20 OUNCES): Calories: 101; Fat: 1.5g; Protein: 7g; Carbohydrates: 15g; Fiber: 0g; Sugar: 15g; Sodium: 209mg

Sweet Red Pepper Broccoli Juice

BONE HEALTH   **BRAIN BOOST**   SKIN CLARITY

SERVES 1 • **PREP TIME:** 15 minutes

Bell peppers, kale, and spinach are known for their high levels of vitamin C and antioxidants, which are essential for eye and gum health. The high amount of vitamin K in broccoli and kale can help speed the healing of bruises, cuts, and wounds. This juice is a delicious way to get boundless energy through its power-house ingredients.

2 large curly kale leaves, deveined

1 cup packed baby spinach

1 cup broccoli florets

1 large red bell pepper, seeded and sectioned

1 large pear, cored

¼ teaspoon ground cumin

1. Rotate the kale, spinach, broccoli, bell pepper, and pear through the juicer.

2. Stir in the cumin, and then drink immediately.

INGREDIENT TIP: Peppers come in different sizes and shapes, including yellow, green, orange, and red. However, red bell peppers pack the most nutrition because they've been on the vine the longest.

PER SERVING (14 TO 18 OUNCES): Calories: 202; Fat: 2g; Protein: 10g; Carbohydrates: 36g; Fiber: 0g; Sugar: 27g; Sodium: 110mg

From left, Green Apple, Spinach, and Avocado Blend (page 74), Green Healing Juice (page 81)

GREEN JUICE

Red Raspberry, Kale, and Lime Splash

BRAIN BOOST   HEART HEALTH   SKIN CLARITY

SERVES 1 • **PREP TIME:** 10 minutes

Raspberries are high in vitamins A, C, and K, and copper, the latter of which is necessary for collagen production to support tissue repair. The combined flavors and nutrients in this juice make it a delicious morning or afternoon green drink.

2 cups raspberries

4 dinosaur kale leaves, deveined

4 celery stalks with leaves

¼ lime, peeled and seeded

Rotate the raspberries, kale, celery, and lime through the juicer. Drink immediately, or refrigerate in an airtight container for up to 24 hours.

INGREDIENT TIP: Kale is a true superfood. It has one of the highest levels of the powerful antioxidant vitamin K (a whopping 684 percent of the recommended daily value). According to a study in *The American Journal of Clinical Nutrition*, a diet rich in vitamin K may reduce your risk for cancer. Anyone taking anticoagulants, such as warfarin, should check with their doctor or pharmacist about eating kale and other dark, leafy green vegetables.

PER SERVING (16 TO 20 OUNCES): Calories: 182; Fat: 2g; Protein: 10g; Carbohydrates: 31g; Fiber: 0g; Sugar: 13g; Sodium: 212mg

Blueberry Spinach Cooler

SERVES 1 • **PREP TIME:** 10 minutes

Spinach is one of the world's most nutritious foods. Loaded with vitamins A and K, it's also high in copper, folate, magnesium, and manganese. Antioxidant-rich blueberries are sweet in flavor, helping make this juice sweet. Iceberg lettuce increases the hydration factor because it is packed with water. Overall, this is a fantastically hydrating, vitamin-rich green juice that your body will love.

2 cups packed baby
  spinach
2 cups packed shredded
  iceberg lettuce
1 cup blueberries
1 celery stalk with leaves

Rotate the spinach, lettuce, blueberries, and celery through the juicer. Drink immediately.

INGREDIENT TIP: If you don't have time to shred the lettuce, feed ½ small head of lettuce through your juicer a couple leaves at a time—it will add up to the same amount. Iceberg lettuce is often overlooked when considering nutritional food, but it is actually packed with important vitamins and minerals. One cup of iceberg lettuce has 20 percent of the recommended daily allowance of vitamin K and 15 percent of vitamin A.

PER SERVING (16 TO 20 OUNCES): Calories: 112; Fat: 0.5g; Protein: 5g; Carbohydrates: 22g; Fiber: 0g; Sugar: 18g; Sodium: 134mg

Strawberry, Collard Greens, and Ginger Juice

ANTI-INFLAMMATORY   CLEANSE AND DETOX   HEART HEALTH

SERVES 1 • **PREP TIME:** 15 minutes

Strawberries provide a big boost of vitamin C, as do collard greens, which are also loaded with vitamin K. Ginger is known for its ability to ease indigestion, but it also has powerful antioxidants and anti-inflammatory properties that add an extra zing to this juice. The flaxseed adds protein and fiber for a mild cleansing effect.

2 cups packed deveined collard green leaves

1 cup strawberries

2 cups packed shredded iceberg lettuce

1 (½-inch) piece fresh ginger

2 teaspoons ground flaxseed

1. Rotate the collard greens, strawberries, lettuce, and ginger through the juicer.

2. Stir in the flaxseed, and then drink immediately.

PER SERVING (16 TO 20 OUNCES): Calories: 90; Fat: 2.5g; Protein: 5g; Carbohydrates: 12g; Fiber: 1g; Sugar: 10g; Sodium: 28mg

Green Apple and Spinach Juice

ANTI-INFLAMMATORY   DIGESTIVE HEALTH   HEART HEALTH

SERVES 1 • **PREP TIME:** 10 minutes

Although you may not be used to apple juice being green, this juice is better than it looks. Made with power-packed ingredients like spinach and celery with the sweetness of apple and carrot, you will be thankful for this simple, uplifting green drink.

2 cups packed baby
  spinach
2 green apples, cored
2 celery stalks with leaves
1 carrot
1 (1-inch) piece fresh
  ginger

Rotate the spinach, apples, celery, carrot, and ginger through the juicer. Drink immediately, or refrigerate in an airtight container for up to 24 hours.

SUBSTITUTION TIP: If you want a slightly different version of this juice, replace the carrot with parsnip, which combines beautifully with the heat of the ginger. You don't need to peel the parsnip, and if it's too large for your juicer's feed chute, simply chop it into large chunks.

PER SERVING (16 TO 20 OUNCES): Calories: 201; Fat: 1g; Protein: 5g; Carbohydrates: 43g; Fiber: 0g; Sugar: 36g; Sodium: 196mg

Blueberry Kale Juice

BRAIN BOOST   CLEANSE AND DETOX   HEART HEALTH

SERVES 1 • **PREP TIME:** 10 minutes

Blueberries are full of healthy vitamins and minerals, which make them an essential element in a detox. They also give this recipe a sweet, fresh flavor. Kale is also a nutritional powerhouse, so when combined with blueberries, this juice becomes a must-have when you need a boost or are feeling a bit under the weather.

---

1 cup blueberries

4 dinosaur kale leaves, deveined

2 romaine lettuce leaves

1 celery stalk with leaves

Rotate the blueberries, kale, lettuce, and celery through the juicer. Drink immediately, or refrigerate in an airtight container for up to 24 hours.

SUBSTITUTION TIP: If dinosaur kale is not available, use curly kale, which is the most common variety found in grocery stores.

PER SERVING (10 TO 14 OUNCES): Calories: 168; Fat: 0.5g; Protein: 8g; Carbohydrates: 33g; Fiber: 0g; Sugar: 15g; Sodium: 122mg

Swiss Chard, Apple, and Fennel Swirl

BONE HEALTH   **DIGESTIVE HEALTH**   **HEART HEALTH**

SERVES 1 • **PREP TIME:** 10 minutes

Swiss chard has one of the broadest arrays of antioxidants of all vegetables. It also contains unique flavonoids called syringic acid that help regulate blood sugar. Fennel is loaded with vitamin C and has an antispasmodic agent that can reduce bloating and cramping. This flavorful green juice is grounding and calming.

2 cups packed Swiss chard leaves and stems

2 fennel bulbs

½ Golden Delicious apple, cored

Leaves from 1 tarragon sprig

3 or 4 cilantro sprigs

Rotate the chard, fennel, apple, tarragon, and cilantro through the juicer. Drink immediately, or refrigerate in an airtight container for up to 24 hours.

HEALTH TIP: The best herbs for any healthy diet are ones you grow yourself, but any produce can be a wonderful addition to your juices. Wash all herbs thoroughly because they grow close to the ground and can be contaminated with bacteria.

PER SERVING (12 TO 16 OUNCES): Calories: 157; Fat: 1g; Protein: 7g; Carbohydrates: 30g; Fiber: 0g; Sugar: 27g; Sodium: 398mg

Green Apple, Spinach, and Avocado Blend

DIGESTIVE HEALTH   HEART HEALTH   SKIN CLARITY

SERVES 1 • **PREP TIME:** 15 minutes

Avocados have anti-inflammatories and antioxidants that promote cardio-vascular health and relief from arthritic pain. Avocados cannot be juiced, so this drink will seem more like a smoothie than a juice. The spinach multiplies the green benefits of this drink, and the green apple adds a slightly tart bite. This juice blend is a satisfying lunch or afternoon drink.

1 Granny Smith apple, cored
2 cups packed baby spinach
½ avocado, peeled and pitted
½ cup spring water
Dash freshly ground black pepper

1. Rotate the apple and spinach through the juicer.

2. In a blender, combine the juice, avocado, water, and pepper. Blend on high speed for 30 seconds, or until smooth. Drink immediately.

TROUBLESHOOTING TIP: To help ripen an avocado, flick off the stem and place the avocado in a brown paper bag on your counter for 1 to 2 days.

PER SERVING (12 TO 16 OUNCES): Calories: 199; Fat: 11g; Protein: 5g; Carbohydrates: 20g; Fiber: 4.5g; Sugar: 16g; Sodium: 94mg

Swiss Chard and Spinach Juice

BRAIN HEALTH   CLEANSE AND DETOX   HEART HEALTH

SERVES 1 • **PREP TIME:** 10 minutes

Swiss chard is one of the greatest natural sources of vitamin K. One cup of Swiss chard contains more than 700 percent of your daily recommended value of vitamin K. This is a lovely green juice to enjoy any time of day.

2 celery stalks with leaves

1 carrot

2 cups packed Swiss chard leaves and stems

½ cup packed baby spinach

Rotate the celery, carrot, chard, and spinach through the juicer. Drink immediately, or refrigerate in an airtight container for up to 24 hours.

INGREDIENT TIP: Swiss chard has not had as much attention as its green counterparts, spinach and kale, but it is packed with health-boosting nutrients. It is very high in vitamin K and an excellent source of vitamins A and C. Store the chard in the fridge in a sealed plastic bag without washing it first because moisture will cause it to spoil faster.

PER SERVING (12 TO 16 OUNCES): Calories: 44; Fat: 0.5g; Protein: 3g; Carbohydrates: 7g; Fiber: 0g; Sugar: 5g; Sodium: 281mg

Sesame Kale Juice

BONE HEALTH   HEART HEALTH   KID FRIENDLY

SERVES 1 • **PREP TIME:** 10 minutes

Raw sesame seeds contain about 5 grams of protein per ¼ cup. They are also a valuable source of monounsaturated fats. This tasty recipe gives you an extra boost by adding a teaspoon of sesame oil to the finished juice.

---

6 kale leaves, deveined

2 celery stalks with leaves

1 romaine lettuce leaf

1 apple, cored

2 tablespoons raw sesame seeds

1 teaspoon sesame oil

1. Rotate the kale, celery, lettuce, and apple through the juicer.

2. Stir in the sesame seeds and sesame oil, and then drink immediately.

TROUBLESHOOTING TIP: Having a hard time getting your kids to drink green juices? The sesame seeds and oil add unique flavors that kids like. They will think sesame kale juice is more of a treat than a green juice!

PER SERVING (12 TO 16 OUNCES): Calories: 358; Fat: 14g; Protein: 13g; Carbohydrates: 45g; Fiber: 2g; Sugar: 20g; Sodium: 194mg

Cucumber, Collard Greens, and Pistachio Juice

ANTI-INFLAMMATORY   BONE HEALTH   HEART HEALTH

SERVES 1 • **PREP TIME:** 15 minutes

Although collard greens contain about 3 grams of protein per 100 grams, you get an extra boost of protein from the pistachios. This juice works well as pre- or post-workout fuel.

4 collard green leaves, deveined

2 carrots

1 cucumber, peeled and halved lengthwise

1 apple, cored

¼ cup shelled pistachios

1. Rotate the collard greens, carrots, cucumber, and apple through the juicer.

2. In a blender, combine the juice and pistachios. Blend on high speed for 30 seconds, or until smooth. Drink immediately, or refrigerate in an airtight container for up to 24 hours.

PER SERVING (16 TO 20 OUNCES): Calories: 364; Fat: 16g; Protein: 15g; Carbohydrates: 40g; Fiber: 3g; Sugar: 31g; Sodium: 126mg

Kale Cabbage Juice

CLEANSE AND DETOX   DIGESTIVE HEALTH   HEART HEALTH

SERVES 1 • **PREP TIME:** 15 minutes

Kale has one of the highest vegetable sources of vitamin K, which is particularly helpful in reducing the risk for certain cancers. Kale is incredibly nutrient dense, containing a variety of vitamins and minerals, including calcium, chlorophyll, iron, and phosphorus. For optimum health, drink this hearty juice whenever you feel under the weather.

1 bunch curly kale, deveined
1 large carrot
½ small head red cabbage
Pinch Chinese five-spice powder

1. Rotate the kale, carrot, and cabbage through the juicer.
2. Stir in the five-spice powder, and then drink immediately, or refrigerate in an airtight container for up to 24 hours.

HEALTH TIP: To create a vegetable stock using the resulting pulp from this recipe, simply combine the pulp with 4 cups of water, 1 cup of fresh herbs of choice, and 1 teaspoon of Chinese five-spice powder in a medium pot. Bring to a boil, and then reduce the heat to medium. Cover and simmer for up to 2½ hours. Strain the stock and discard the pulp. Let cool, and then refrigerate in an airtight container for up to 2 weeks.

PER SERVING (14 TO 18 OUNCES): Calories: 215; Fat: 3g; Protein: 15g; Carbohydrates: 32g; Fiber: 0g; Sugar: 19g; Sodium: 217mg

Kickin' Kale Collard Green Juice

ANTI-INFLAMMATORY BONE HEALTH HEART HEALTH

SERVES 2 • **PREP TIME:** 15 minutes

Kale is an incredibly versatile vegetable. In combination with the antioxidant content of collard greens, the kale in this juice provides excellent anti-cancer benefits. This juice will have you upping your daily green intake while feeling the heat from the ginger for a day of high-yield productivity.

1 bunch curly kale,
  deveined (2 cups)
1 bunch collard green
  leaves, deveined (2 cups)
2 large stalks celery with
  leaves
1 (1-inch) piece fresh
  ginger

Rotate the kale, collard greens, celery, and ginger through the juicer. Drink immediately, or refrigerate in an airtight container for up to 24 hours.

PER SERVING (10 TO 14 OUNCES): Calories: 86; Fat: 2g; Protein: 9g; Carbohydrates: 8g; Fiber: 0g; Sugar: 4g; Sodium: 98mg

Royal Green

BONE HEALTH   BRAIN BOOST   SKIN CLARITY

SERVES 1 • **PREP TIME:** 15 minutes

With their high levels of antioxidants, like copper and vitamins C and K, pears promote healthy complexions. Your skin loves antioxidants because they protect your body from potential free-radical damage. The simple ingredients in this juice are mild and palatable, leaving a satisfying feeling in your tummy.

1 pear, cored

3 cups packed baby spinach

1 cucumber, peeled and halved lengthwise

½ lemon, peeled, seeded, and sectioned

1 (½-inch) piece fresh ginger

Rotate the pear, spinach, cucumber, lemon, and ginger through the juicer. Drink immediately, or refrigerate in an airtight container for up to 24 hours.

HEALTH TIP: Cucumbers provide a wonderful way to cool and calm irritated skin. Pour some pure cucumber juice into a spray bottle and spritz it on your face. Keep refrigerated for up to 4 days.

PER SERVING (14 TO 18 OUNCES): Calories: 140; Fat: 0.5g; Protein: 6g; Carbohydrates: 28g; Fiber: 0g; Sugar: 21g; Sodium: 136mg

Green Healing Juice

BRAIN BOOST **HEART HEALTH** **SKIN CLARITY**

SERVES 1 • **PREP TIME:** 15 minutes

The classic green juice is a blend of leafy greens that purify your cells. Cucumber hydrates, and herbs detoxify and brighten your appearance. My version contains half the fruit and twice the greens for a potent dose of healing energy.

2 cups packed baby
  spinach
3 kale leaves, deveined
½ cucumber, peeled and
  halved lengthwise
1 green apple, cored
2 tablespoons chopped
  fresh cilantro
½ lime with the rind,
  seeded and sectioned
1 (½-inch) piece fresh
  ginger

Rotate the spinach, kale, cucumber, apple, cilantro, lime, and ginger through the juicer. Drink immediately, or refrigerate in an airtight container for up to 24 hours.

TROUBLESHOOTING TIP: Some people with a certain gene variation involved in sensing smells think cilantro tastes like soap. If this sounds like you, substitute curly parsley.

PER SERVING (16 TO 20 OUNCES): Calories: 170; Fat: 2g; Protein: 10g; Carbohydrates: 28g; Fiber: 0g; Sugar: 20g; Sodium: 146mg

Happy Face Green Juice

SERVES 1 • **PREP TIME:** 10 minutes

Did you know that what you put into your body reflects in your skin? Food has been used to support skin issues and make skin glow for ages. In this recipe, I turn to carrots to promote an even skin tone and turmeric root for its anti-inflammatory and antibacterial benefits. Glowing, clear skin brings more self-confidence to your day.

6 carrots

1 bunch romaine lettuce, chopped (2 cups)

2 celery stalks

1 orange, peeled, seeded, and sectioned

1 (1-inch) piece fresh ginger

1 (1-inch) piece fresh turmeric

Rotate the carrots, lettuce, celery, orange, ginger, and turmeric through the juicer. Drink immediately, or refrigerate in an airtight container for up to 2 days.

HEALTH TIP: Carrot pulp makes a great facial mask for any skin type. Stir together 3 to 4 tablespoons of honey and ¼ cup of carrot pulp and apply the mixture to your face. Leave on for 10 minutes, and then rinse. If the paste is too thick, add 1 to 2 teaspoons of carrot juice.

PER SERVING (16 TO 20 OUNCES): Calories: 197; Fat: 1.5g; Protein: 6g; Carbohydrates: 40g; Fiber: 0g; Sugar: 32g; Sodium: 325mg

Sparkling Blackberry Green Juice

SERVES 1 • **PREP TIME:** 10 minutes

As you drink this juice, close your eyes and imagine yourself at a spa, sipping on a healing elixir. The blackberries help your body reduce inflammation and fight infection, while the collard greens encourage a youthful glow.

½ cup blackberries

4 large collard green leaves, deveined

½ lime, seeded

8 ounces sparkling mineral water

1. Rotate the blackberries, collard greens, and lime through the juicer.

2. Stir the juice into the sparkling mineral water, and then drink immediately.

INGREDIENT TIP: The peak season for blackberries is late summer. Stock up on these beauties when they are on sale, put them in the freezer, and then thaw before use.

PER SERVING (14 TO 18 OUNCES): Calories: 73; Fat: 1.5g; Protein: 7g; Carbohydrates: 8g; Fiber: 0g; Sugar: 4g; Sodium: 35mg

Wheatgrass Supreme

ANTI-INFLAMMATORY   BONE HEALTH   HEART HEALTH

SERVES 1 • **PREP TIME:** 15 minutes

Wheatgrass has a powerful, earthy flavor that does, in fact, taste like grass. That might not sound appealing, but the orange and apple in this recipe make the juice sweeter. Adding wheatgrass to your diet is a great idea because it is one of the best sources of chlorophyll, which supports the purification of your blood. Enjoy this juice as a morning cocktail to supercharge your day.

---

1 handful wheatgrass

1 cucumber, peeled and halved lengthwise

2 cups packed baby spinach

1 orange, peeled, seeded, and sectioned

1 Granny Smith apple, cored

1. Juice the wheatgrass.

2. Rotate the cucumber, spinach, orange, and apple through the juicer. Drink immediately.

TROUBLESHOOTING TIP: Wheatgrass, a young, sprouted grass, does not contain gluten, though it is a type of wheat plant. Gluten is found only in the seed kernels of the wheat plant, so wheatgrass is safe to consume if you follow a gluten-free diet.

PER SERVING (16 TO 20 OUNCES): Calories: 173; Fat: 1g; Protein: 6g; Carbohydrates: 35g; Fiber: 0g; Sugar: 31g; Sodium: 93mg

Green Protein Power

ANTI-INFLAMMATORY   BRAIN BOOST   HEART HEALTH

SERVES 1 • **PREP TIME:** 15 minutes

After a workout, you need a healthy treat that will provide hydration, improve your recovery, and enhance your performance. Kale and chard leaves contain protein, and you can add your own plant-based protein powder to this juice for an extra boost.

1 cup cubed pineapple

5 kale leaves, deveined

3 chard leaves, deveined

1 cucumber, peeled and halved lengthwise

2 scoops plant-based protein powder

1. Rotate the pineapple, kale, chard, and cucumber through the juicer.

2. In a blender, combine the juice and protein powder. Blend on high speed for 30 seconds, or until smooth. Drink immediately.

INGREDIENT TIP: When choosing a plant-based protein powder, make sure protein is the first ingredient listed on the label. It's also a good idea to select a brand with a plant-based sweetener, like stevia.

PER SERVING (18 TO 22 OUNCES): Calories: 202; Fat: 2g; Protein: 22g; Carbohydrates: 24g; Fiber: 0.5g; Sugar: 4g; Sodium: 513mg

Alkalizing Greens

ANTI-INFLAMMATORY   **BRAIN BOOST**   **HEART HEALTH**

SERVES 1 • **PREP TIME:** 15 minutes

Your body seeks homeostasis, or balance. A body that measures more alkaline tends to be healthier. Processed foods lower alkalinity and make your body more acidic. Drink this juice to stay alkaline and on point to maintain a healthy lifestyle.

2 cups packed baby
  spinach
1 cucumber, peeled and
  halved lengthwise
1 cup broccoli florets
2 kale leaves, deveined
1 Granny Smith apple,
  cored
1 lemon with rind, seeded
  and sectioned

Rotate the spinach, cucumber, broccoli, kale, apple, and lemon through the juicer. Drink immediately, or refrigerate in an airtight container for up to 2 days.

HEALTH TIP: In addition to drinking alkaline juices, regular aerobic exercise, such as a brisk walk, helps restore the pH balance in your body by increasing your metabolism.

PER SERVING (16 TO 20 OUNCES): Calories: 189; Fat: 1g; Protein: 10g; Carbohydrates: 35g; Fiber: 0g; Sugar: 22g; Sodium: 153mg

Green for the Gold

CLEANSE AND DETOX   DIGESTIVE HEALTH   SKIN CLARITY

SERVES 2 • **PREP TIME:** 10 minutes

This highly nutritious energy drink is packed with antioxidants that help the mind and body function at optimum levels. Pear and cucumber go well together for hydration and fighting free radicals, and the vitamin C in spinach promotes skin health. This juice will give you the feeling of winning a gold medal.

3 cups packed baby spinach

1 cucumber, peeled and halved lengthwise

1 small golden beet

2 pears, cored

1 teaspoon ground turmeric

½ teaspoon spirulina powder

1 teaspoon ground flaxseed

1. Rotate the spinach, cucumber, beet, and pears through the juicer.

2. Stir in the turmeric, spirulina, and flaxseed, and then drink immediately, or refrigerate in an airtight container for up to 24 hours.

INGREDIENT TIP: Make sure to eat the peel of the pear, as it has up to six times more polyphenols than the flesh. Polyphenols are powerful antioxidants that can help prevent or even reverse damage in your cells from aging, environment, or lifestyle.

PER SERVING (16 TO 20 OUNCES): Calories: 189; Fat: 1g; Protein: 10g; Carbohydrates: 35g; Fiber: 0g; Sugar: 22g; Sodium: 153mg

**Carrot Orange Juice,
page 91**

CHAPTER 5

IMMUNE BOOSTER

Ginger Beet Juice

SERVES 1 • **PREP TIME:** 10 minutes

Ginger not only helps relax the intestinal tract, but it also helps reduce gas. In many cultures, ginger has been used as an herbal remedy to relieve nausea. A little goes a long way, though, so don't use more than is specified. Prepare this juice when you need a little extra peace and calm in your belly.

3 kale leaves, deveined
1 beet
1 carrot
1 apple, cored
1 (1-inch) piece fresh ginger

Rotate the kale, beet, carrot, apple, and ginger through the juicer. Drink immediately, or refrigerate in an airtight container for up to 2 days.

PER SERVING (12 TO 16 OUNCES): Calories: 196; Fat: 0.5g; Protein: 7g; Carbohydrates: 41g; Fiber: 0g; Sugar: 27g; Sodium: 169mg

Carrot Orange Juice

DIGESTIVE HEALTH   HEART HEALTH   KID FRIENDLY

SERVES 1 • **PREP TIME:** 10 minutes

If you are used to starting your mornings with a glass of orange juice, this recipe won't be too much of a stretch. The carrots enhance the sunny color and add beta-carotene to an already healthy juice. Carrots can also help regulate blood sugar even though they have a glycemic index of 80. In addition to this juice's high nutrient and vitamin levels, it's a health-giving glass of sunshine.

4 carrots

1 orange, peeled, seeded, and sectioned

1 apple, cored

Rotate the carrots, orange, and apple through the juicer. Drink immediately, or refrigerate in an airtight container for up to 24 hours.

INGREDIENT TIP: Carrots might become your ingredient of choice for many juicing recipes because they add a satisfying sweetness, blend well with other ingredients, and are inexpensive. If budget is not a huge concern, try juicing carrots in all the different colors available to see the range of gorgeous results. The flavor won't change regardless of the carrot's color.

PER SERVING (12 TO 16 OUNCES): Calories: 221; Fat: 1g; Protein: 4g; Carbohydrates: 49g; Fiber: 0g; Sugar: 43g; Sodium: 170mg

Bountiful Beet Juice

ANTI-INFLAMMATORY   CLEANSE AND DETOX   HEART HEALTH

SERVES 2 • **PREP TIME:** 20 minutes

Beets are known for their nutritional value. What many people do not realize is that beet greens are just as healthy. One cup of beet greens contains 3 grams of protein. Beet greens have a mild, sweet flavor and are loaded with vitamin C to help support your immune system.

1 small golden beet
1 small red beet
2 cups chopped beet greens
1 apple, cored
½ cucumber, peeled and halved lengthwise
½ lemon, peeled, seeded, and sectioned

Rotate the golden and red beets, beet greens, apple, cucumber, and lemon through the juicer. Drink immediately, or refrigerate in an airtight container for up to 2 days.

INGREDIENT TIP: Betalain, a highly bioactive pigment in both golden and red beets, has high anti-inflammatory and antioxidant properties. Not many vegetables have betalain–go beets!

PER SERVING (10 TO 14 OUNCES): Calories: 84; Fat: 0.5g; Protein: 2g; Carbohydrates: 18g; Fiber: 0g; Sugar: 17g; Sodium: 152mg

Ginger Blast

ANTI-INFLAMMATORY　BRAIN BOOST　DIGESTIVE HEALTH

SERVES 1 • **PREP TIME:** 15 minutes

This homemade version of ginger ale is a great stomach tonic and a refreshing drink for any occasion. Spinach gives an extra immune boost, and cherries are great for reducing inflammation, especially if you suffer from arthritis. This is a refreshing, invigorating juice for any health enthusiast.

1½ cups packed baby
 spinach
1 cup cherries, pitted
1 (1-inch) piece fresh
 ginger
1 cup sparkling water

1. Rotate the spinach, cherries, and ginger through the juicer.

2. Stir the juice into the sparkling water, and then drink immediately.

INGREDIENT TIP: True sparkling water contains minerals and is obtained from an underground source. The water takes in minerals from the layers of natural rock it flows through. I recommend buying sparkling water brands that contain minerals without added flavors or sugars.

PER SERVING (14 TO 18 OUNCES): Calories: 108; Fat: 0.5g; Protein: 3g; Carbohydrates: 23g; Fiber: 0g; Sugar: 20g; Sodium: 65mg

Immunity Plus

ANTI-INFLAMMATORY DIGESTIVE HEALTH HEART HEALTH

SERVES 1 • **PREP TIME:** 15 minutes

When your immune system is strong, your body can more easily fight off viral infections and chronic ailments. Antioxidants like vitamin C are key factors in building your immune system, and this juice is packed with nutritious ingredients and antioxidants to keep you healthy.

1 small beet
2 carrots
8 celery stalks
1 broccoli stalk, peeled
2 garlic cloves, peeled

Rotate the beet, carrots, celery, broccoli stalk, and garlic through the juicer. Drink immediately.

HEALTH TIP: For more than 5,000 years, garlic has been used as food and medicine. Scientists believe that garlic has antiviral properties that strengthen the immune system and block the entry of viruses into cells.

PER SERVING (14 TO 18 OUNCES): Calories: 133; Fat: 1.5g; Protein: 8g; Carbohydrates: 22g; Fiber: 0g; Sugar: 18g; Sodium: 436mg

Vitamin C Celebration

ANTI-INFLAMMATORY **BRAIN BOOST** **HEART HEALTH**

SERVES 1 • **PREP TIME:** 15 minutes

Vitamin C is needed by every part of your body to grow and repair tissue. When consumed regularly, vitamin C helps build your immune system so viral colds stay away. Drink this juice often for its healing vibes and sweet, citrusy flavor.

1 orange, peeled, seeded, and sectioned

½ red bell pepper, seeded

1 cup broccoli florets

2 collard green leaves, deveined

¼ cucumber, peeled and halved lengthwise

Rotate the orange, bell pepper, broccoli, collard greens, and cucumber through the juicer. Drink immediately, or refrigerate in an airtight container for up to 24 hours.

INGREDIENT TIP: Red bell peppers are actually green bell peppers that have remained on the plant to ripen. The red peppers contain twice the amount of vitamin C as green bell peppers and taste sweeter, which makes them more popular for juicing and eating raw.

PER SERVING (14 TO 18 OUNCES): Calories: 109; Fat: 1g; Protein: 7g; Carbohydrates: 18g; Fiber: 0g; Sugar: 17g; Sodium: 39mg

Beta-Carotene Greens

SERVES 1 • **PREP TIME:** 15 minutes

Carrots and dark, leafy greens are high in beta-carotene, which the body converts into vitamin A. Your skin, mucous membranes, immune system, and vision require this vitamin for optimal health. Drink this rich juice to give you energy and stamina all day.

4 Swiss chard leaves, deveined

4 kale leaves, deveined

4 carrots

1 green bell pepper, seeded

1 lemon, peeled, seeded, and sectioned

Rotate the chard, kale, carrots, bell pepper, and lemon through the juicer. Drink immediately, or refrigerate in an airtight container for up to 2 days.

INGREDIENT TIP: Eating carrots may help improve eyesight in low-light conditions, research shows. Carrots contain beta-carotene, a pigment that nourishes the eye and helps the body make vitamin A. Vitamin A, in turn, allows the eye to transmit light as a signal to the brain, allowing people to see under low-light conditions.

PER SERVING (16 TO 20 OUNCES): Calories: 225; Fat: 1g; Protein: 13g; Carbohydrates: 41g; Fiber: 0g; Sugar: 18g; Sodium: 662mg

Triple Berry Tonic

ANTI-INFLAMMATORY KID FRIENDLY SKIN CLARITY

SERVES 2 • **PREP TIME:** 10 minutes

This recipe includes the trifecta of fresh berries: blueberries, raspberries, and strawberries. Berries are low in calories and high in nutrients and help fight inflammation. To add a festive mood to your Triple Berry Tonic, add a splash of sparkling water.

2 large romaine lettuce leaves

2 cups blueberries

1 cup raspberries

1 cup strawberries

1 large celery stalk with leaves

Splash sparkling water (optional)

1. Rotate the lettuce, blueberries, raspberries, strawberries, and celery through the juicer.

2. Add a splash of sparkling water (if using). Drink immediately, or refrigerate in an airtight container for up to 2 days.

INGREDIENT TIP: For a thicker juice, use frozen blueberries. In a blender, combine the juice with the frozen blueberries. Blend on high speed for 30 seconds, or until smooth.

PER SERVING (12 TO 16 OUNCES): Calories: 121; Fat: 1g; Protein: 2g; Carbohydrates: 26g; Fiber: 0g; Sugar: 21g; Sodium: 22mg

Liven Up Your Liver Juice

CLEANSE AND DETOX   DIGESTIVE HEALTH   SKIN CLARITY

SERVES 2 • **PREP TIME:** 15 minutes

Even the pretty color of this juice will make your liver smile. Beets contain many nutrients that help detoxify the liver and kidneys, making beets an excellent choice for digestive health. This juice is packed with as much flavor as nutrition and will keep you coming back for more.

2 medium red beets
2 carrots
1 apple, cored
1 (1-inch) piece fresh ginger
¼ teaspoon ground cinnamon

1. Rotate the beets, carrots, apple, and ginger through the juicer.

2. Stir in the cinnamon, and then drink immediately, or refrigerate in an airtight container for up to 24 hours.

SUBSTITUTION TIP: An Asian pear is a cross between an apple and a pear. It's a great source of dietary fiber and helps the digestive system maintain a healthy level of good bacteria. In this recipe, you can swap the apple for an Asian pear.

PER SERVING (10 TO 14 OUNCES): Calories: 92; Fat: 0.5g; Protein: 2g; Carbohydrates: 20g; Fiber: 0g; Sugar: 18g; Sodium: 107mg

Cleansing Cocktail

ANTI-INFLAMMATORY   **BRAIN BOOST**   **SKIN CLARITY**

SERVES 2 • **PREP TIME:** 15 minutes

Cabbage is traditionally used as a cleanser for your digestive tract. Broccoli's high vitamin and mineral levels are best absorbed from its raw form. The high concentration of phytonutrients in broccoli contributes to the cleansing properties of this potent cocktail. If you like spice, throw in a jalapeño pepper for a fiesta in a glass!

1 head broccoli, cut into florets, stalks saved for another use

2 green bell peppers, seeded

½ head green cabbage

2 tomatoes, sectioned

Rotate the broccoli, bell peppers, cabbage, and tomatoes through the juicer. Drink immediately.

PER SERVING (10 TO 14 OUNCES): Calories: 96; Fat: 0.5g; Protein: 6g; Carbohydrates: 17g; Fiber: 0g; Sugar: 16g; Sodium: 82mg

Collagen Juice

SERVES 2 • **PREP TIME:** 20 minutes

Brussels sprouts are known for their anticancer, anti-inflammation, and detox-ification properties. The ingredients in this juice will also boost your skin's appearance. You may need to add a splash of water to cut the strength of the flavor a little. Also, stir in ½ teaspoon of freshly ground black pepper if you'd like to zing it up.

6 Brussels sprouts, bases
  trimmed
1 beet
½ head green cabbage
1 red bell pepper, seeded
1 head broccoli, cut into
  florets, stalks saved, for
  another use

Rotate the Brussels sprouts, beet, cabbage, bell pepper, and broccoli through the juicer. Drink immediately, or refrigerate in an airtight container for up to 24 hours.

PER SERVING (10 TO 14 OUNCES): Calories: 104; Fat: 0.5g; Protein: 7g; Carbohydrates: 18g; Fiber: 0g; Sugar: 16g; Sodium: 121mg

Radical Red Bell Pepper Juice

BRAIN BOOST   DIGESTIVE HEALTH   HEART HEALTH

SERVES 2 • **PREP TIME:** 15 minutes

Vitamins C and E are classified as antioxidants, and these two nutrients are available in abundance in bell peppers. In fact, a bell pepper has more vitamin C than an orange. This immunity-boosting juice also boosts your mood with its vibrant color.

2 red bell peppers, cored and seeded

1 cup packed shredded red cabbage

1 celery stalk with leaves

1 carrot

1 apple, cored

Rotate the bell peppers, cabbage, celery, carrot, and apple through the juicer. Drink immediately, or refrigerate in an airtight container for up to 24 hours.

TROUBLESHOOTING TIP: Non-organic bell peppers seem to have a surprising amount of pesticide residue remaining on them. To ensure the freshest, purest bell pepper, buy organic.

PER SERVING (10 TO 14 OUNCES): Calories: 88; Fat: 0.5g; Protein: 2g; Carbohydrates: 19g; Fiber: 0g; Sugar: 17g; Sodium: 52mg

Blueberry Blast

ANTI-INFLAMMATORY   **KID FRIENDLY**   **SKIN CLARITY**

SERVES 1 • **PREP TIME:** 10 minutes

Berries and cucumber are one of my favorite combinations. The high water content in cucumber promotes hydration while liquifying this juice to a perfect consistency. The mellow cucumber flavor lets the berries take center stage for a tasty, high-antioxidant juice.

1 cup blackberries

1 cup blueberries

1 cucumber, peeled and halved lengthwise

Rotate the blackberries, blueberries, and cucumber through the juicer. Drink immediately, or refrigerate in an airtight container for up to 24 hours.

HEALTH TIP: Purple or darker berries, like blackberries and blueberries, have as much as 50 percent more antioxidants than lighter-colored berries.

PER SERVING (14 TO 18 OUNCES): Calories: 137; Fat: 1.5g; Protein: 4g; Carbohydrates: 27g; Fiber: 0g; Sugar: 24g; Sodium: 7mg

Watermelon Basil Juice

ANTI-INFLAMMATORY   BONE HEALTH   DIGESTIVE HEALTH

SERVES 1 • **PREP TIME:** 15 minutes

Watermelon is rich in arginine and vitamins A and C. These immune-boosting vitamins are high in antioxidants and can also relieve muscle soreness, which makes this a nutritious after-workout drink. Additionally, the striking red color of this juice can bring energy and excitement to your day.

2 cups chopped watermelon
6 fresh basil leaves

Rotate the watermelon and basil through the juicer. Drink immediately.

INGREDIENT TIP: To juice or not to juice the watermelon rind? The rind is a great source of the amino acid citrulline, which is a natural immune booster. As an option, make this recipe with the rind on. The juice won't be as sweet, but it will contain more nutrition per glass.

PER SERVING (16 TO 20 OUNCES): Calories: 96; Fat: 0.5g; Protein: 2g; Carbohydrates: 21g; Fiber: 0g; Sugar: 19g; Sodium: 3mg

Jamu Juice Tonic

ANTI-INFLAMMATORY   **HEART HEALTH**   **SKIN CLARITY**

SERVES 2 • **PREP TIME:** 10 minutes

Jamu is a powerful and traditional Indonesian medicine drink made from two main ingredients: turmeric and ginger. It is a natural anti-inflammatory, immune-boosting, beautifying drink. I've added pineapple and coconut water to this classic recipe to make it more palatable, hydrating, and energizing.

1 (2-inch) piece fresh turmeric

1 (1-inch) piece fresh ginger

½ lemon with rind, seeded and sectioned

1 cup cubed pineapple

2 cups unsweetened unflavored coconut water

½ teaspoon freshly ground black pepper

1. Rotate the turmeric, ginger, lemon, and pineapple through the juicer.

2. Stir together the juice, coconut water, and pepper. Drink immediately, or refrigerate in an airtight container for up to 2 days.

INGREDIENT TIP: Pineapple is not traditionally used in jamu. I find the refreshing sweetness of pineapple goes well with this spicy, medicinal classic.

PER SERVING (12 TO 16 OUNCES): Calories: 92; Fat: 0g; Protein: 1g; Carbohydrates: 22g; Fiber: 0g; Sugar: 18g; Sodium: 64mg

Green Immunity Juice

BRAIN BOOST   KID FRIENDLY   SKIN CLARITY

SERVES 2 • **PREP TIME:** 10 minutes

Spirulina is grown in fresh and salt water and is typically known as blue-green algae. It is a superfood that may be the single most nutritious food on the planet. Spirulina benefits both the body and brain through its high levels of antioxidants, B vitamins, copper, iron, protein, and the list goes on. If you need an extra boost of immunity to ward off viruses, Green Immunity Juice will do the job.

1 cup cubed pineapple

1 cup blueberries

2 cups packed baby spinach

1 (3.5-ounce) packet frozen unsweetened acai

1½ teaspoons spirulina

1 teaspoon cacao powder

1. Rotate the pineapple, blueberries, and spinach through the juicer.

2. In a blender, combine the juice, acai, spirulina, and cacao powder. Blend on high speed for 30 seconds, or until smooth. Drink immediately, or refrigerate in an airtight container for up to 2 days.

TROUBLESHOOTING TIP: Since the acai is frozen, this juice consistency will be thicker. If it is too thick for your liking, add a splash of water, but not so much that you water down the potency.

PER SERVING (10 TO 14 OUNCES): Calories: 132; Fat: 4g; Protein: 4g; Carbohydrates: 20g; Fiber: 2g; Sugar: 15g; Sodium: 76mg

Tomato and Spinach Juice

BONE HEALTH   **BRAIN BOOST**   HEART HEALTH

SERVES 1 • **PREP TIME:** 10 minutes

Heirloom tomatoes come in a variety of shapes and colors—from small and red to large yellow, green, and even purple. These tomatoes contain lycopene, a kind of carotenoid that plays a role in the prevention of cancer and a powerful natural antioxidant that protects the skin from harmful UV rays. The lemon adds a fresh, citrusy taste that awakens your body and mind.

---

2 cups packed baby spinach
2 large heirloom tomatoes
½ lemon with rind, seeded and sectioned

Rotate the spinach, tomatoes, and lemon through the juicer. Drink immediately, or refrigerate in an airtight container for up to 24 hours.

TROUBLESHOOTING TIP: Never store tomatoes in the refrigerator! Refrigerating a tomato destroys its flavor and creates a mushy texture. Store cut tomatoes in a sealed airtight container at room temperature for up to 24 hours.

PER SERVING (16 TO 20 OUNCES): Calories: 80; Fat: 0.5g; Protein: 6g; Carbohydrates: 13g; Fiber: 0g; Sugar: 11g; Sodium: 106mg

Red Refresher

SERVES 1 • **PREP TIME:** 20 minutes

This is delicious, refreshing, and fabulous for you, plus the color is beautiful. Punicalagin, a potent antioxidant in pomegranates, gets high praise for having an antioxidant level three times higher than green tea. Red Refresher is packed with vitamins and minerals for a potent immunity-boosting juice.

1 small red beet
Seeds of 1 pomegranate
1 cup diced watermelon

Rotate the beet, pomegranate seeds, and watermelon through the juicer. Drink immediately.

PER SERVING (16 TO 20 OUNCES): Calories: 210; Fat: 2g; Protein: 5g; Carbohydrates: 43g; Fiber: 0g; Sugar: 41g; Sodium: 50mg

Cherry Apple Chiller

BRAIN BOOST DIGESTIVE HEALTH **HEART HEALTH**

SERVES 1 • **PREP TIME:** 15 minutes

Antioxidants are compounds that protect you and your cells from free radicals, or harmful molecules that can contribute to chronic conditions. Apples are high in vitamins C and E, contributing to their many health benefits. Great for everyday juicing or for serving to guests, this juice packs a nutritional punch that's hard to beat. Add the fact that it tastes wonderful, and you have a hit!

2 mint sprigs

2 Granny Smith apples, cored

1 cup sour cherries, pitted

2 ounces seltzer water

1. Rotate the mint, apples, and cherries through the juicer.

2. Stir the juice into the seltzer water, and then drink immediately, or refrigerate in an airtight container for up to 24 hours.

SUBSTITUTION TIP: For a more tropical, high-electrolyte juice, substitute unsweetened unflavored coconut water for the seltzer water.

PER SERVING (16 TO 20 OUNCES): Calories: 229; Fat: 1g; Protein: 3g; Carbohydrates: 52g; Fiber: 0g; Sugar: 45g; Sodium: 8mg

Tomato Veggie Juice

BONE HEALTH **BRAIN BOOST** CLEANSE AND DETOX

SERVES 2 • **PREP TIME:** 15 minutes

What better way to start your day than with a glass full of healthy nutrients? This Tomato Veggie Juice is packed with antioxidants, vitamins, and minerals from A to Z. It tastes like a fresh salad in a glass.

2 medium tomatoes

2 celery stalks with leaves

1 cup packed shredded romaine lettuce

1 red bell pepper, cored and seeded

1 carrot

½ cup fresh parsley

Rotate the tomatoes, celery, lettuce, bell pepper, carrot, and parsley through the juicer. Drink immediately, or refrigerate in an airtight container for up to 2 days.

INGREDIENT TIP: Parsley is known as one of the most powerful disease-fighting plants. It is rich in vitamin K, which is needed for bone health, and also high in vitamins A and C. Italian flat-leaf and French curly leaf parsley are the two most common types. Use either variety for this recipe.

PER SERVING (10 TO 14 OUNCES): Calories: 52; Fat: 0.5g; Protein: 3g; Carbohydrates: 9g; Fiber: 0g; Sugar: 8g; Sodium: 72mg

**Good, Good,
Good Digestion,**
page 120

CHAPTER 6

CLEANSE AND DETOX

Spinach Orange Juice

ANTI-INFLAMMATORY   DIGESTIVE HEALTH   HEART HEALTH

SERVES 1 • **PREP TIME:** 15 minutes

Spinach is one of the most potent natural sources of the antioxidant lutein. It also contains high levels of beta-carotene and zeaxanthin. Some people avoid large quantities of spinach because it contains oxalic acid, which is thought to prevent the absorption of calcium and iron. Oxalic acid undergoes a change when cooked, which can create absorption issues, but raw spinach juice does not have this effect.

2 cups packed baby spinach

1 navel orange, peeled, seeded, and sectioned

1 celery stalk with leaves

1 cucumber, peeled and halved lengthwise

Rotate the spinach, orange, celery, and cucumber through the juicer. Drink immediately.

PER SERVING (14 TO 18 OUNCES): Calories: 132; Fat: 0.5g; Protein: 5g; Carbohydrates: 27g; Fiber: 0g; Sugar: 15g; Sodium: 123mg

Cranberry Kale Juice

BRAIN HEALTH   CLEANSE AND DETOX   HEART HEALTH

SERVES 1 • **PREP TIME:** 15 minutes

Cranberries contain only 44 calories per cup and are naturally low in sugar. Combined with nutrient-rich kale, this recipe becomes a low-calorie wonder. This delightfully tart juice will give you a gentle cleanse with mighty vitamins, including A, C, and K.

4 kale leaves, deveined
2 celery stalks with leaves
2 romaine lettuce leaves
1 cup cranberries
½ lemon, peeled, seeded, and sectioned

Rotate the kale, celery, lettuce, cranberries, and lemon through the juicer. Drink immediately, or refrigerate in an airtight container for up to 24 hours.

TROUBLESHOOTING TIP: This juice has a very intense tart taste that will make your mouth water. To cut the tartness a little, add a few fresh raspberries or strawberries to the mix.

PER SERVING (14 TO 18 OUNCES): Calories: 132; Fat: 0.5g; Protein: 7g; Carbohydrates: 25g; Fiber: 0g; Sugar: 6g; Sodium: 155mg

Spicy Apple Detox Tonic

ANTI-INFLAMMATORY　**CLEANSE AND DETOX**　DIGESTIVE HEALTH

SERVES 2 • **PREP TIME:** 15 minutes

If you think you know apple juice, think again. This spicy apple tonic is like no apple juice you've ever tried. The pectin in apples helps movement through your digestive tract. Drink it once and you'll never go back to plain apple juice.

4 large apples, cored
2 large celery stalks
1 cup packed baby spinach
1 (½-inch) piece fresh ginger
Pinch cayenne pepper

1. Rotate the apples, celery, spinach, and ginger through the juicer.

2. Stir in the cayenne, and then drink immediately, or refrigerate in an airtight container for up to 24 hours.

PER SERVING (12 TO 16 OUNCES): Calories: 225; Fat: 1g; Protein: 2g; Carbohydrates: 52g; Fiber: 0g; Sugar: 47g; Sodium: 77mg

Cran-Raspberry Spritzer

CLEANSE AND DETOX   HEART HEALTH   SKIN CLARITY

SERVES 2 • **PREP TIME:** 15 minutes

Did you know cranberries are nearly 90 percent water? Their high water content makes cranberries a top choice for cleansing. The added citrus boosts immunity, aids iron absorption, and promotes healthy, glowing skin.

2 cups cranberries

1 medium navel orange, peeled, seeded, and sectioned

1 lime, peeled, seeded, and sectioned

½ cup raspberries

2 to 3 tablespoons sparkling water

1. Rotate the cranberries, orange, lime, and raspberries through the juicer.

2. Stir in the sparkling water, and then drink immediately, or refrigerate in an airtight container for up to 2 days.

INGREDIENT TIP: There are many varieties of lime, including desert lime, key lime, makrut lime, and Persian lime. All limes, no matter the variety, are high in vitamin C and antioxidants.

PER SERVING (10 TO 14 OUNCES): Calories: 80; Fat: 0.5g; Protein: 1g; Carbohydrates: 18g; Fiber: 0g; Sugar: 12g; Sodium: 2mg

Anti-Inflammatory Juice

ANTI-INFLAMMATORY   BONE HEALTH   DIGESTIVE HEALTH

SERVES 1 • **PREP TIME:** 10 minutes

Research shows that chronic inflammation is likely a common factor in heart disease and autoimmune disorders. The ingredients in this juice, which contain vitamin K and antioxidants, protect against oxidative stress and help reduce inflammation. Spinach and carrots are both high in antioxidants and loaded with vitamin K. Enjoy this cleansing, upbeat, healthy juice.

1 cup packed baby spinach

4 carrots

2 celery stalks

1 Granny Smith apple, cored

½ teaspoon ground cinnamon

1. Rotate the spinach, carrots, celery, and apple through the juicer.

2. Stir in the cinnamon, and then drink immediately, or refrigerate in an airtight container for up to 2 days.

SUBSTITUTION TIP: In addition to cinnamon, other spices known to reduce inflammation include cayenne pepper, clove, cumin, ginger, rosemary, sage, and turmeric. For variety, try a pinch of one of these spices in place of cinnamon.

PER SERVING (14 TO 18 OUNCES): Calories: 177; Fat: 1g; Protein: 5g; Carbohydrates: 37g; Fiber: 0.5g; Sugar: 28g; Sodium: 277mg

Timeless Beauty Juice

BRAIN BOOST CLEANSE AND DETOX SKIN CLARITY

SERVES 1 • **PREP TIME:** 20 minutes

The small amount of extra time it takes to make this juice is worth the effort. Artichokes contribute to healthy collagen development and the appearance of younger-looking skin. For that reason, you'll often find artichoke extract in luxury skin care products.

1 artichoke (see tip)
1 green apple, cored
1 cup packed baby
  spinach
1 celery stalk

Rotate the artichoke, apple, spinach, and celery through the juicer. Drink immediately.

PREPARATION TIP: It's easy to prepare an artichoke for this recipe. Remove the stem from the artichoke, trim 1 to 2 inches off the top, and cut it into small pieces. Press down on the center of the artichoke to open the leaves and rinse well under running water to remove any trapped dirt. Halve the artichoke and scoop out the hairy center with a grapefruit spoon. Tear or cut away the leaves.

PER SERVING (10 TO 14 OUNCES): Calories: 132; Fat: 0.5g; Protein: 6g; Carbohydrates: 26g; Fiber: 0g; Sugar: 18g; Sodium: 197mg

Clear Skin Juice

BONE HEALTH   <mark>CLEANSE AND DETOX</mark>   <mark>SKIN CLARITY</mark>

SERVES 2 • **PREP TIME:** 15 minutes

Each ingredient in this recipe promotes healthy skin. Carrots boost collagen production, lemons brighten skin, and broccoli provides a healthy glow. Turmeric root reduces redness, and inflammation and the detoxifying mustard greens add a spicy kick. Get ready to show off your glowingly clear skin!

8 carrots

4 mustard green leaves

3 lemons, peeled and seeded

2 cups broccoli florets

1 (½-inch) piece fresh turmeric

Rotate the carrots, mustard greens, lemons, broccoli, and turmeric through the juicer. Drink immediately, or refrigerate in an airtight container for up to 24 hours.

INGREDIENT TIP: You can choose from many varieties of mustard greens—from curly to flat in shape and green to purple in color. In spring, you also may notice that mustard green leaves are smaller and more tender.

PER SERVING (12 TO 16 OUNCES): Calories: 141; Fat: 1.5g; Protein: 7g; Carbohydrates: 25g; Fiber: 0g; Sugar: 17g; Sodium: 207mg

Antioxidant Supreme

ANTI-INFLAMMATORY BONE HEALTH HEART HEALTH

SERVES 1 • **PREP TIME:** 15 minutes

If you think all green juices taste the same, prepare to be surprised. This juice has an intriguing yet mellow flavor. Blackberries give this juice an incredible dark-green color, while the fennel adds potassium, magnesium, calcium, and a flavorful twist.

4 kale leaves, deveined
½ cup blackberries
½ green apple, cored
1 cup broccoli florets
1 cucumber, peeled and halved lengthwise
½ fennel bulb

Rotate the kale, blackberries, apple, broccoli, cucumber, and fennel through the juicer. Drink immediately, or refrigerate in an airtight container for up to 24 hours.

INGREDIENT TIP: Save the fennel stalks and fronds. Think of fennel fronds (the leafy parts) as herbs and use them in salads, marinades, and soups. You can substitute the stalks for celery in most recipes.

PER SERVING (14 TO 18 OUNCES): Calories: 205; Fat: 1.5g; Protein: 12g; Carbohydrates: 36g; Fiber: 0g; Sugar: 20g; Sodium: 167mg

Good, Good, Good Digestion

BONE HEALTH   DIGESTIVE HEALTH   SKIN CLARITY

SERVES 1 • **PREP TIME:** 15 minutes

Good digestion is critical to your overall health. Some people believe disease originates in the gut, so when you treat your digestive tract well, you're treating your entire body. Papaya contains wonderful enzymes that do the trick when it comes to digestion. This juice treats your digestive system with respect and kindness for good health.

1 cup cubed papaya

6 kale leaves, deveined

1 (1-inch) piece fresh
  turmeric

1 lemon, peeled, seeded,
  and sectioned

Rotate the papaya, kale, turmeric, and lemon through the juicer. Drink immediately, or refrigerate in an airtight container for up to 24 hours.

INGREDIENT TIP: Papain, the main enzyme in papaya, aids digestion by breaking down proteins into smaller fragments and by allowing greater absorption of vitamins and minerals. And it adds a fresh, tropical taste to juices and smoothies.

PER SERVING (10 TO 14 OUNCES): Calories: 196; Fat: 0.5g; Protein: 10g; Carbohydrates: 38g; Fiber: 0g; Sugar: 13g; Sodium: 134mg

The Delicious Green Cleanse

CLEANSE AND DETOX   DIGESTIVE HEALTH   SKIN CLARITY

SERVES 1 • **PREP TIME:** 15 minutes

This attractive green drink is as good for you as it looks. Fortunately, it tastes refreshing and pleasant while working hard to fight disease and detoxify your body. Each ingredient works well independently, but together they create a powerhouse. If this drink tastes too rich, add a little more cucumber to thin the juice, which will only help make your skin clear and bright.

1 green bell pepper, seeded

½ cup broccoli florets

1 cucumber, peeled and halved lengthwise

1 cup shredded green cabbage

Rotate the bell pepper, broccoli, cucumber, and cabbage through the juicer. Drink immediately, or refrigerate in an airtight container for up to 24 hours.

PER SERVING (12 TO 16 OUNCES): Calories: 56; Fat: 0.5g; Protein: 4g; Carbohydrates: 9g; Fiber: 0g; Sugar: 8g; Sodium: 32mg

Cabbage Soup Juice

SERVES 1 • **PREP TIME:** 15 minutes

Rich in vegetables that help your body detoxify and flush toxins, this juice is both delicious and nutritious. Garlic is a natural full-body detoxifying ingredient that delivers antiviral and antibacterial qualities and was even used in ancient Egypt for its health and therapeutic benefits.

1 cup shredded green cabbage

2 garlic cloves, peeled

6 to 8 fresh basil leaves

2 tomatoes, sectioned

1 green bell pepper, seeded

Rotate the cabbage, garlic, basil, tomatoes, and bell pepper through the juicer. Drink immediately, or refrigerate in an airtight container for up to 24 hours.

HEALTH TIP: Did you know cabbage is a powerful detoxifying agent and weight loss aid that makes a great base anytime you want to prepare a cleansing juice? The basil and green pepper are packed with chlorophyll, so you're getting good oxygen flow in addition to all the health benefits of the other vegetables.

PER SERVING (14 TO 18 OUNCES): Calories: 76; Fat: 0.5g; Protein: 4g; Carbohydrates: 14g; Fiber: 0g; Sugar: 11g; Sodium: 32mg

Apple Juice Detox

SERVES 1 • **PREP TIME:** 15 minutes

This recipe is light and delicious but is also a cleansing powerhouse. Mint leaves have medicinal properties that help with digestive issues, bloating, and stomach pains. The delicious combination of ingredients in this juice make this cleansing detox a tasty treat.

2 Granny Smith apples, cored

¼ cup fresh mint leaves

1 lemon with rind, seeded and sectioned

1 orange, peeled, seeded, and sectioned

1 cucumber, peeled and halved lengthwise

Rotate the apples, mint, lemon, orange, and cucumber through the juicer. Drink immediately, or refrigerate in an airtight container for up to 24 hours.

INGREDIENT TIP: Apples have been used for centuries as a natural detoxifier. Malic acid is a substance found naturally in apples that is cleansing and promotes skin hydration.

PER SERVING (14 TO 18 OUNCES): Calories: 245; Fat: 1g; Protein: 4g; Carbohydrates: 55g; Fiber: 0g; Sugar: 49g; Sodium: 11mg

Leafy Green Delight

SERVES 1 • **PREP TIME:** 15 minutes

The greens in this juice provide a veritable cocktail of vitamins and minerals. This is an ideal combination for detoxing and colon cleansing. This juice is best to drink first thing in the morning to let all of the nutrients, vitamins, and detoxifying ingredients absorb fully on an empty stomach. This gentle cleanse will have you feeling clear, energized, and peaceful.

6 kale leaves, deveined

1 cup packed baby spinach

1 cup deveined collard green leaves

1 green bell pepper, seeded

1 garlic clove, peeled

Rotate the kale, spinach, collard greens, bell pepper, and garlic through the juicer. Drink immediately, or refrigerate in an airtight container for up to 24 hours.

PER SERVING (12 TO 16 OUNCES): Calories: 164; Fat: 0.5g; Protein: 13g; Carbohydrates: 27g; Fiber: 0g; Sugar: 3g; Sodium: 176mg

Headache Cure

BONE HEALTH **BRAIN BOOST** SKIN CLARITY

SERVES 1 • **PREP TIME:** 15 minutes

Magnesium, vitamin C, and calcium are necessary to get rid of a headache. You may be dehydrated as well, so drink a big glass (or two!) of water with this. If your headache persists, drink another glass of juice. If you need a hydrating pick-me-up, this is a health-conscious juice for everyone.

1 cup cauliflower florets

1 cup broccoli florets

1 apple, cored

1 orange, peeled, seeded, and sectioned

Rotate the cauliflower, broccoli, apple, and orange through the juicer. Drink immediately.

INGREDIENT TIP: Broccoli is a good hangover and headache cure because it's rich in magnesium, calcium, and vitamin C—all things your body craves when it's trying to recover from dehydration.

PER SERVING (12 TO 16 OUNCES): Calories: 185; Fat: 1g; Protein: 6g; Carbohydrates: 38g; Fiber: 0g; Sugar: 34g; Sodium: 53mg

Broccoli Beet Juice

ANTI-INFLAMMATORY   CLEANSE AND DETOX   HEART HEALTH

SERVES 2 • **PREP TIME:** 15 minutes

Beets are rich in phytonutrients called betalains, which not only provide anti-oxidant and anti-inflammatory benefits but also help detoxify the body. These phytonutrients are particularly beneficial for liver detoxification. You can also add the beet greens to this juice for an extra cleanse and detox.

2 golden beets

2 broccoli stalks, peeled

2 celery stalks with leaves

1 carrot

1 orange, peeled, seeded, and sectioned

½ lemon, peeled, seeded, and sectioned

Rotate the beets, broccoli, celery, carrot, orange, and lemon through the juicer. Drink immediately, or refrigerate in an airtight container for up to 2 days.

SUBSTITUTION TIP: To dramatically change the color of the juice to red and give it a more earthy taste, use red beets instead of golden beets. You will receive the same liver detoxification benefits.

PER SERVING (8 TO 12 OUNCES): Calories: 96; Fat: 0.5g; Protein: 5g; Carbohydrates: 18g; Fiber: 0g; Sugar: 17g; Sodium: 149mg

Bell Pepper and Purple Cabbage Splash

BRAIN BOOST DIGESTIVE HEALTH **HEART HEALTH**

SERVES 1 • **PREP TIME:** 15 minutes

This juice combines the best of both the unripe (green) and ripe (red) versions of bell pepper. Bell peppers are high in folate and vitamins A, B_6, and C, and they blend well with the mild cabbage taste and the fresh flavor of the celery. In this recipe, juice the celery greens for extra detoxing, as they contain five times more magnesium and calcium than the celery stalks.

1 green bell pepper, cored and seeded

1 red bell pepper, cored and seeded

2 cups packed shredded purple cabbage

4 celery stalks with leaves

Rotate the green and red bell peppers, cabbage, and celery through the juicer. Drink immediately, or refrigerate in an airtight container for up to 24 hours.

PER SERVING (16 TO 20 OUNCES): Calories: 101; Fat: 1g; Protein: 5g; Carbohydrates: 18g; Fiber: 0g; Sugar: 15g; Sodium: 174mg

Pineapple Cherry Punch

DIGESTIVE HEALTH   KID FRIENDLY   SKIN CLARITY

SERVES 1 • **PREP TIME:** 15 minutes

Banish free radicals with this fruity punch. Plums contain twice the amount of antioxidants as other popular fruits, such as nectarines and peaches. One medium plum has about 30 calories and is loaded with vitamin C. Like apples, plums are rich in pectin, which helps food move through the colon effectively. Drink this juice when you want more clarity of mind, luminous skin, and a clear colon.

1 cup cubed pineapple
2 plums
1 cup sour cherries, pitted

Rotate the pineapple, plums, and cherries through the juicer. Drink immediately, or refrigerate in an airtight container for up to 2 days.

PER SERVING (14 TO 18 OUNCES): Calories: 217; Fat: 1g; Protein: 3g; Carbohydrates: 49g; Fiber: 0g; Sugar: 42g; Sodium: 6mg

Pomegranate Cherry Juice

ANTI-INFLAMMATORY   CLEANSE AND DETOX   HEART HEALTH

SERVES 2 • **PREP TIME:** 20 minutes

Drink your arthritis away with this juice rich in anti-inflammatories. The nitrates found in beets help with inflammatory conditions like rheumatoid arthritis and fibromyalgia. Beets are also known for keeping your digestive system regular. The detox results from drinking this juice will have you feeling lighter and more energetic.

2 golden beets
½ cup blackberries
Seeds of 1 pomegranate
½ cup sour cherries, pitted
2 kiwis, peeled and
  sectioned

Rotate the beets, blackberries, pomegranate seeds, cherries, and kiwis through the juicer. Drink immediately, or refrigerate in an airtight container for up to 2 days.

SUBSTITUTION TIP: If you don't have kiwis, substitute 1 cup of strawberries and a dash of lime juice. Strawberries are similar in texture, have seeds like kiwis, and are also high in vitamin C and antioxidants.

PER SERVING (10 TO 14 OUNCES): Calories: 165; Fat: 1.5g; Protein: 4g; Carbohydrates: 34g; Fiber: 0g; Sugar: 31g; Sodium: 68mg

Restore and Regenerate

ANTI-INFLAMMATORY · CLEANSE AND DETOX · DIGESTIVE HEALTH

SERVES 2 · **PREP TIME:** 10 minutes

This restoring and nurturing juice gently cleanses with the low-calorie hydrating properties of cucumber. Its mild flavor makes it a favorite cleansing ingredient. This juice is a balanced blend of flavors, vitamins, and minerals.

4 kale leaves, deveined
1 cup packed baby spinach
2 cucumbers, peeled and halved lengthwise
1 cup blueberries
1 lime with the rind, seeded and sectioned
1 teaspoon spirulina
1 tablespoon ground flaxseed

1. Rotate the kale, spinach, cucumbers, blueberries, and lemon through the juicer.

2. Stir in the spirulina and flaxseed, and then drink immediately, or refrigerate in an airtight container for up to 24 hours.

SUBSTITUTION TIP: Substitute cranberries for the blueberries, as both berries have high antioxidant levels and are beneficial for preventing and treating urinary tract infections. They both contain the antioxidant proanthocyanidin (PAC), and D-mannose, which help prevent bacteria from sticking to the walls of the urinary tract.

PER SERVING (12 TO 16 OUNCES): Calories: 129; Fat: 1.5g; Protein: 7g; Carbohydrates: 22g; Fiber: 0.5g; Sugar: 11g; Sodium: 85mg

Sweet Parsley Apple Tonic

ANTI-INFLAMMATORY BONE HEALTH DIGESTIVE HEALTH

SERVES 2 • **PREP TIME:** 15 minutes

This recipe is a sweet, pleasant-tasting, and cleansing juice. The harmony among ginger and turmeric and parsley and apple creates a fresh spicy, tart, sweet taste. Loaded with vitamins and minerals, like vitamins C and K and calcium, this juice delivers a nutritionally satisfying cleanse.

1 cup fresh parsley

4 celery stalks with leaves

2 Granny Smith apples, cored

1 lime with rind, seeded and sectioned

1 (1-inch) piece fresh ginger

1 (1-inch) piece fresh turmeric

Rotate the parsley, celery, apples, lime, ginger, and turmeric through the juicer. Drink immediately, or refrigerate in an airtight container for up to 24 hours.

INGREDIENT TIP: Gingerol is the compound in ginger responsible for its spicy flavor and healing properties. Gingerol can improve issues like inflammatory bowel disease, arthritis, and the common cold. Ginger and turmeric together have been proven to be more effective as anti-inflammatory healers.

PER SERVING (10 TO 14 OUNCES): Calories: 109; Fat: 1g; Protein: 2g; Carbohydrates: 23g; Fiber: 0g; Sugar: 17g; Sodium: 83mg

Measurement Conversions

VOLUME EQUIVALENTS	U.S. STANDARD	U.S. STANDARD (OUNCES)	METRIC (APPROXIMATE)
LIQUID	2 tablespoons	1 fl. oz.	30 mL
	¼ cup	2 fl. oz.	60 mL
	½ cup	4 fl. oz.	120 mL
	1 cup	8 fl. oz.	240 mL
	1½ cups	12 fl. oz.	355 mL
	2 cups or 1 pint	16 fl. oz.	475 mL
	4 cups or 1 quart	32 fl. oz.	1 L
	1 gallon	128 fl. oz.	4 L
DRY	⅛ teaspoon	–	0.5 mL
	¼ teaspoon	–	1 mL
	½ teaspoon	–	2 mL
	¾ teaspoon	–	4 mL
	1 teaspoon	–	5 mL
	1 tablespoon	–	15 mL
	¼ cup	–	59 mL
	⅓ cup	–	79 mL
	½ cup	–	118 mL
	⅔ cup	–	156 mL
	¾ cup	–	177 mL
	1 cup	–	235 mL
	2 cups or 1 pint	–	475 mL
	3 cups	–	700 mL
	4 cups or 1 quart	–	1 L
	½ gallon	–	2 L
	1 gallon	–	4 L

WEIGHT EQUIVALENTS

U.S. STANDARD	METRIC (APPROXIMATE)
½ ounce	15 g
1 ounce	30 g
2 ounces	60 g
4 ounces	115 g
8 ounces	225 g
12 ounces	340 g
16 ounces or 1 pound	455 g

Resources

Books

Gilbert, Mary Esther, MSc HN, BSc NSP. *Potent Superfoods for Lifelong Health: Over 100 Proven Botanicals—Complete Cellular Nourishment—Optimizing the Body's Protective Capacity*

The collection of superfoods and natural medicines in this book reflects decades of ever-increased knowledge of the power of superfoods.

Reinhard, Tonia. *Superfoods: The Healthiest Foods on the Planet*

Registered dietitian Tonia Reinhard gives expert advice in this easy-to-use guide on the two hundred very best high-powered superfoods.

Companies That Specialize in Superfoods

• healthforcesuperfoods.com

• livingtreecommunityfoods.com

• navitasorganics.com

• sunfood.com

References

Best Health (blog). "Soothe Nausea with Ginger—A Dietary Supplement That Works." October 21, 2015. besthealthmag.ca/article/soothe-nausea-with-ginger -a-dietary-supplement-that-works.

Beswick, Kyle. "What Are Electrolytes?" *Cedars-Sinai* (blog). October 16, 2019. cedars-sinai.org/blog/electrolytes.html.

Brown, Jessica. "The 6 Best Brain Foods to Eat as You Age." *Prevention*. December 18, 2017. prevention.com/health/a20511072/best-foods-brain-health.

Brown, Mary Jane. "Juicing: Good or Bad?" October 4, 2019. healthline.com/nutrition/ juicing-good-or-bad.

Crocker, Pat. "A Brief History of Juicing." March 25, 2016. dummies.com/article/ home-auto-hobbies/food-drink/juicing-smoothies/a-brief-history-of -juicing-142786.

Frew, Lucy. "All Disease Begins in the Gut." *Be Well Magazine*. January 12, 2019. invitationtohealth.com.au/be-well-magazine/all-disease-begins-in -the-gut.

Georgina, Chanel. "How to Live Longer: Lead an Anti-Inflammatory Lifestyle—Here's How." *The Express*. November 21, 2020. express.co.uk/life-style/health/1362826/ how-to-live-longer-anti-inflammatory-lifestyle.

Goodnature (blog) "Who is Norman Walker?" October 10, 2019. goodnature.com/blog/ norwalk-closes-its-doors.

Goodson, Amy. "Why Turmeric and Black Pepper Is a Powerful Combination." Healthline. July 4, 2018. healthline.com/nutrition/turmeric-and-black-pepper.

Haupt, Angela. "Health Benefits of Spirulina." *Forbes*. December 10, 2021. forbes.com/health/body/health-benefits-of-spirulina.

Kaminska, Karolina. "Arthritis: Eat These Three Delicious Fruits to Soothe Arthritis Pain and Symptoms." *The Express*. October 29, 2018. express.co.uk/life-style/health/1037851/arthritis-pain-rheumatoid-arthritis-knee-symptoms-diet-avocado-watermelon-grapes.

Lang, Ariane. "Is Wheatgrass Gluten-Free?" Healthline. April 30, 2020. healthline.com/nutrition/is-wheatgrass-gluten-free.

The Nutrition Source (blog). "Kale." 2022. hsph.harvard.edu/nutritionsource/food-features/kale.

Petre, Alina. "Lycopene: Health Benefits and Top Food Sources." Healthline. October 3, 2018. healthline.com/nutrition/lycopene.

Raman, Ryan. "12 Healthy Foods High in Antioxidants." Healthline. March 12, 2018. healthline.com/nutrition/foods-high-in-antioxidants.

Reuters Health (blog). "Higher Vitamin K Intake Tied to Lower Cancer Risks." March 31, 2010. reuters.com/article/health-us-vitamin-k/higher-vitamin-k-intake-tied-to-lower-cancer-risks-idUKTRE62U4VO20100331.

Sass, Cynthia. "3 Great Reasons to Snack on Pecans, According to a Nutritionist." *Yahoo News*. October 30, 2017. yahoo.com/news/3-great-reasons-snack-pecans-202233592.html.

Stiles, Laura. "Blueberries May Help Prevent Effect of Alzheimer's." PsychiatryAdvisorcom. March 14, 2016. psychiatryadvisor.com/home/topics/neurocognitive-disorders/alzheimers.

Index

ACKNOWLEDGMENTS

I want to give a big thank-you to Yoshita and Ariel at Callisto Media—your belief in me and constant inspiration are truly a gift. To my editor, Leah Zarra, my books shine and sparkle with your magic touch; thank you so much!

To all the organic farmers who work tirelessly planting, cultivating, and picking their crops with intention and care, I thank you, and appreciate and respect the valuable work you do.

To all of you who have made juicing part of your life: You are changing your connection to the planet, Mother Nature, and the sincere relationship to your mind-body connection. Thank yourself for setting an example of love, patience, and happiness through the simple act of juicing.

ABOUT THE AUTHOR

 **Nora Day** is the author of *A Year of Meditation*, *A Year of Abundance*, and *3-Ingredient Juicing Recipe Book* and is also a teacher and an inspirational speaker and advocate of living an abundant lifestyle. She is the founder of YogiNora.com, a one-stop subscription site for yoga classes, guided meditations, and plant-based juicing and smoothie recipes. With more than 85,000 subscribers and more than 6 million views across YouTube, Facebook, and Instagram, Nora is a sought-after wellness expert. She embodies a lifestyle of yoga, meditation, juicing, plant-based living, and peaceful abundance in her formula for well-being, longevity, and happiness. Visit her website for more information: NoraDayLive.com.

CPSIA information can be obtained
at www.ICGtesting.com
Printed in the USA
BVHW020915260622
640507BV00002BA/5

9 781638 077916